budgetbooks

PIANO / VOCAL / GUITAR

CHRISTMAS SONGS

ISBN 0-634-04743-4

7777 W. BLUEMOUND RD. P.O. BOX 13819 MILWAUKEE, WI 53213

Visit Hal Leonard Online at
www.halleonard.com

CONTENTS

ALL I WANT FOR CHRISTMAS IS YOU

Words and Music by MARIAH CAREY
and WALTER AFANASIEFF

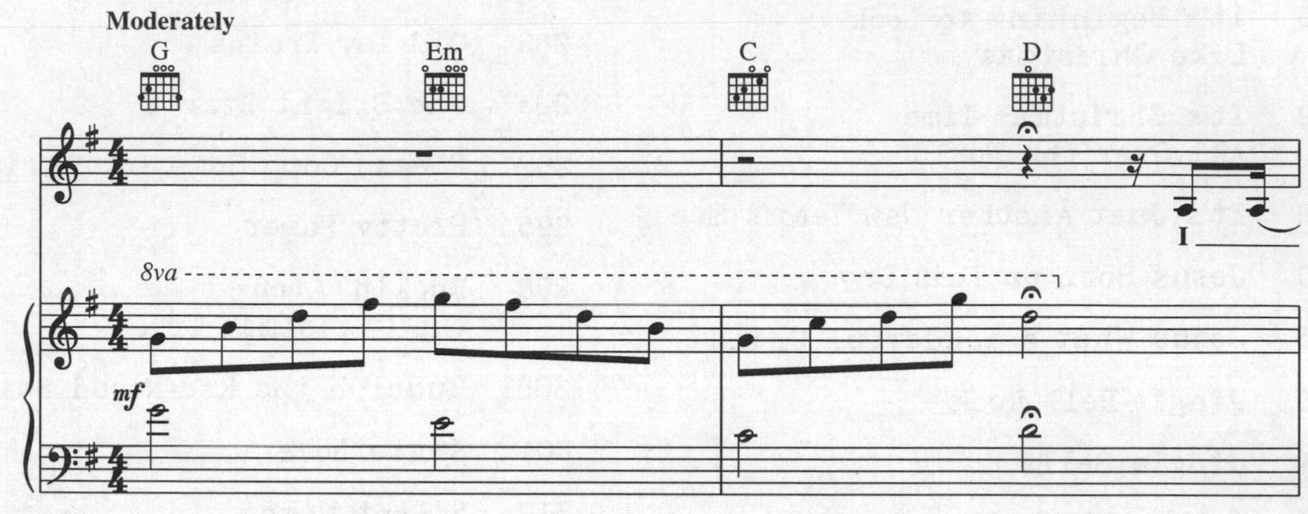
Moderately
G
Em
C
D
I
8va
mf

Rubato
G
G/B
3
don't want a lot for Christ-mas, there is just one thing I need.
loco

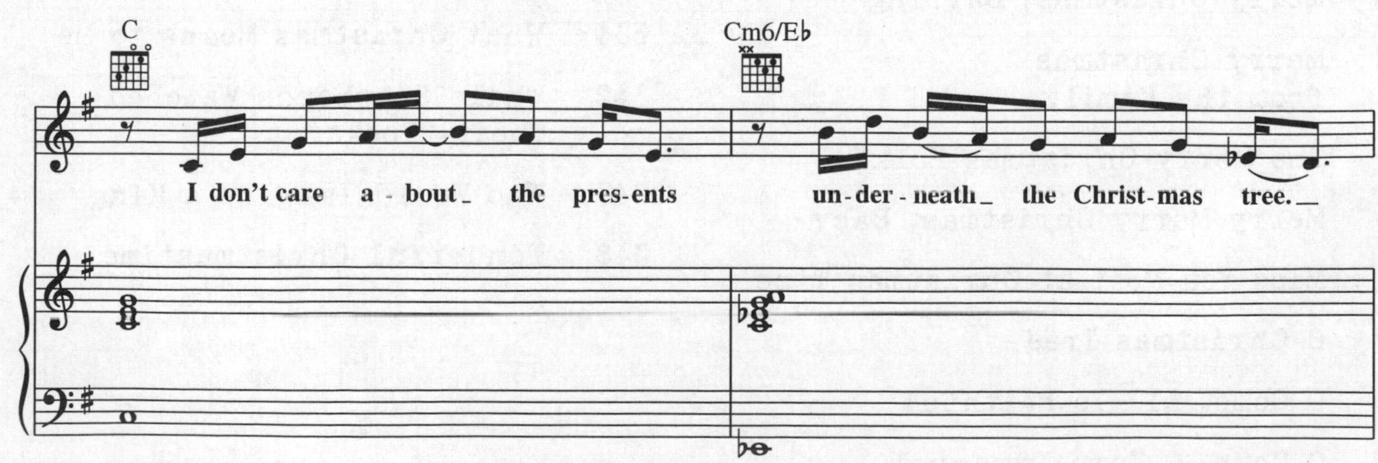
C
Cm6/E♭
I don't care a - bout the pres-ents un-der-neath the Christ-mas tree.

G/D
B7♯5
Em
Cm6/E♭
I just want you for my own, more than you __ could ev - er know.
G/D
E7
Am7
Am7♭5/D
3 fr
Make my wish come true: __ all I __ want for Christ-mas is you, __
G
Moderately fast
Em
C
D
yeah. __

G
I don't want a lot for Christ-mas, there is just one thing
I won't ask for much this Christ-mas, I won't e - ven wish
C
I need And I don't care a - bout the pres - ents,
for snow. And I, I'm just gon - na keep on wait-ing
Cm6/E♭
un - der - neath the Christ - mas tree.
un - der - neath the mis - tle - toe.
G
I don't need to hang my stock - ing there up - on the fi -
I won't make a list and send it to the North Pole for
I don't want a lot for Christ - mas, this is all I'm ask -

C
- re - place.
Saint Nick.
- ing for.
San - ta Claus won't make me hap - py
I won't e - ven stay a - wake to
I just want to see my ba - by
Cm6/E♭
with a toy on Christ - mas day
hear those mag - ic rein - deer click.
stand - ing right out - side my door.
G
B7
Em
I just want you for my own,
I just want you here to - night,
I just want him for my own,
more than you could ev
hold - ing on to me
more than you could ev -
Cm6/E♭
G/D
- er know.
so tight.
- er know.
Make my wish come true:
What more can I do?
Make my wish come true:

E7
To Coda
Am9
Am7♭5/D
3fr
all I want for Christ - mas is
Ba - by all I want for Christ - mas is
G
Em
Am9
you.
you.
You,
You,
3
3
3
3
1
D7
2
D7
B7
ba - by. Oh,
ba - by. Oh,
All the lights
Em
are shin - ing so bright - ly ev - 'ry - where,

B7
Em
and the sound of chil - dren's laugh - ter fills the air,
Cm6/E♭
And ev - 'ry - one is sing - ing.
G/D
E7
Am9
I hear those sleigh bells ring - ing.
San - ta won't you please bring me
D7
D.S. al Coda
what I real - ly need, won't you please bring my ba - by to me.
Oh,

CODA
Am7
Am7♭5/D
3 fr
all I want for Christ - mas
is
you.
G
Em
Am9
D7
G
Ooh, ba - by.
All I want for
Em
Am9
D7
Repeat and Fade
Christ - mas is you, ba - by.

AS LONG AS THERE'S CHRISTMAS

from Walt Disney's BEAUTY AND THE BEAST - THE ENCHANTED CHRISTMAS

Music by RACHEL PORTMAN
Lyrics by DON BLACK

Flowing
B♭
E♭
3fr
Cm
3fr
mf
F
Dm7
E♭(add9)
B♭/D
Cm
3fr
Female: There is more to this time of year
Gm/B♭
A♭
4fr
E♭/G
3fr
G♭
than sleigh - bells and hol - ly, Male: mis - tle - toe and
Freely
D♭/F
B♭/F
Cm7/F
F
snow. Both: Those things will come and go. Female: Don't look

Tempo I
B♭
Cm/B♭
B♭
F/B♭
in - side a stock - ing. Don't look un - der the tree. The
B♭(add9)/D
E♭
Cm7
F
one thing we're look - ing for is some-thing we can't see. Male: Far more
B♭
Cm/B♭
B♭
pre - cious than sil - ver and more splen - did than
F/B♭
B♭/D
F/E♭
E♭
gold, this is some - thing to trea - sure, but it's

Cm7 B♭/D B♭/E♭ Fsus F B♭ B♭/D
some - thing we can't hold. Oh. Both: As long as there's
E♭ Cm7 F F/E♭ B♭/D
Christ-mas, I tru - ly be - lieve Male: that hope is the
E♭ B♭/F Fsus F B♭
great - est Both: of the gifts we'll re - ceive, Male: we'll re - ceive.
D♭ E♭m/D♭
As we all pray to - geth - er, it's a

D♭
A♭/D♭
B♭m7
A♭
G♭
time to re - joice. Female: And though we may look dif - f'rent, Both: we'll
E♭m7
A♭sus
A♭/G♭
Fsus
all sing with one voice. Male: Whoa.
F
B♭
B♭/D
E♭
Both: As long as there's Christ - mas, I
Cm7
F
F/E♭
B♭/D
F/E♭
E♭
tru - ly be - lieve that hope is the great - est great - est of the

Bb/F
Fsus
F
Bb
Eb
3 fr
gifts we'll re - ceive. _ As long as there's Christ-mas, we'll
Cm7
F
F/Eb
Bb/D
all be just fine. A star shines a - bove us, _ Female: light-ing
Gb
Ab/Gb
4 fr
your way Male: and mine. _
Db/F
Bbm7
Amaj7
Female: Oh. _
Male: Light _ my way. Female: You know I will. _

C#m7
4fr
F#7
B
B/D#
4fr
Both: As long as there's
poco rall.
a tempo
E
B/D#
4fr
C#m7
4fr
F#
F#/E
B/D#
4fr
Christ-mas, I tru - ly be - lieve that hope is the
E
B/F#
F#
great - est of the gifts we'll re - ceive. As
B
D#m7
E
C#m7
4fr
F#
long as our our guid - ing star shines a - bove, there'll

B/D#
4fr
E
al - ways be Christ - mas,
Male: so there
B/D#
4fr
C#m7
4fr
B/F#
F#7sus
3
al - ways will be a time
Both: when the world is filled with peace and
C#m/B
B
E
C#m7
4fr
F#
love.
B/D#
4fr
E
C#m7
4fr
E/F#
F#7
B
rit.

ANGELS FROM THE REALMS OF GLORY

Words by JAMES MONTGOMERY
Music by HENRY T. SMART

Joyfully
C
An - gels from the
F
C/E
Am
G7
C
realms of glo - ry, Wing your flight o'er all the earth,
Ye who sang cre -
E
Am
E7
Am
G/D
D7
G
G7
a - tion's sto - ry, Now pro - claim Mes - si - ah's birth.
Come and wor - ship!

C7 F Dm C/E Dm/F Am G7 C
Come and wor - ship! Wor - ship Christ the new - born King! Sa - ges, leave your
C/G G7 C F C Am G7 C
con - tem - pla - tions, Bright - er vis - ions beam a - far, Seek the great De -
C/G G7 C E Am E Am G/D D7 G G7
sire of na - tions Ye have seen His__ na - tal star. Come and wor - ship!
C C7 F Dm C/E Dm/F D7/F# G7sus G7 C
Come and wor - ship! Wor - ship Christ the new - born King!

ANGELS WE HAVE HEARD ON HIGH

Traditional French Carol
Translated by JAMES CHADWICK
Moderately
mp
F Am Csus C F C F
An - gels we have heard on high Sweet - ly sing - ing
F/C C7 F Am Csus C F
o'er the plains, And the moun - tains in re - ply
C F F/C C7 F D
Ech - o - ing their joy - ous strains. Glo -

Gm C Fmaj7 B♭ C C7
- - - - - - - - - ri - a
F C F B♭ F/C C F D
in ex - cel - sis De - o, Glo - -
Gm C Fmaj7 B♭ C C7
- - - - - - - - - ri - a.
F C F B♭ F/C C7 F
in ex - cel - sis De - o

Am
Csus
C
F
Shep - herds, why this ju - bi - lee?
C
F
F/C
C7
F
Why your joy - ous strains pro - long?
Am
Csus
C
F
What the glad - some tid - ings be
C
F
F/C
C7
F
D
Which in - spire your heaven - ly song? Glo - - -

Gm C Fmaj7 B♭ C C7

- - - - - - ri - a

F C F B♭ F/C C F D

in ex - cel - sis De - o, Glo - - -

Gm C Fmaj7 B♭ C C7

- - - - - - - ri - a

F C F B♭ F/C C7 F

in ex - cel - sis De - o.

AS WITH GLADNESS MEN OF OLD

Words by WILLIAM CHATTERTON DIX
Music by CONRAD KOCHER

Moderate tempo
Db Cm7 Abm Bbm7 Ab Eb7 Ab Ab Db/F
As with glad - ness
As with joy - ful
Bbm7 Eb7 Ab Dbmaj7 Ab/Eb Eb7 Ab
men of old Did the guid - ing star be - hold;
steps they sped To that low - ly man - ger bed,
Db Bbm7 Eb7 Ab
As with joy the hailed its light,
there to bend the knee be - fore

Dbmaj7
Ab/Eb
Eb7
Ab
Lead - ing on - ward beam - ing bright;
Him whom heav'n and earth a - bove
Gmb5/Bb
Ab/C
Eb7
Ab
So, most gra - cious Lord, may we
So, may we with will - ing feet
Db
Cm7
Abm
Bbm7
Ab
Eb7
Ab
Ev - er - more be led to Thee.
Ev - er seek Thy mer - cy seat.

3. As they offered gifts most rare,
So may we with holy joy,
All our costliest treasures bring,
At that manger rude and bare,
Pure and free from sin's alloy,
Christ, to Thee, our heav'nly King.

AWAY IN A MANGER

Traditional
Music by JAMES R. MURRAY

Sweetly
mp
A -

F
B♭
way in a man - ger, no crib for a

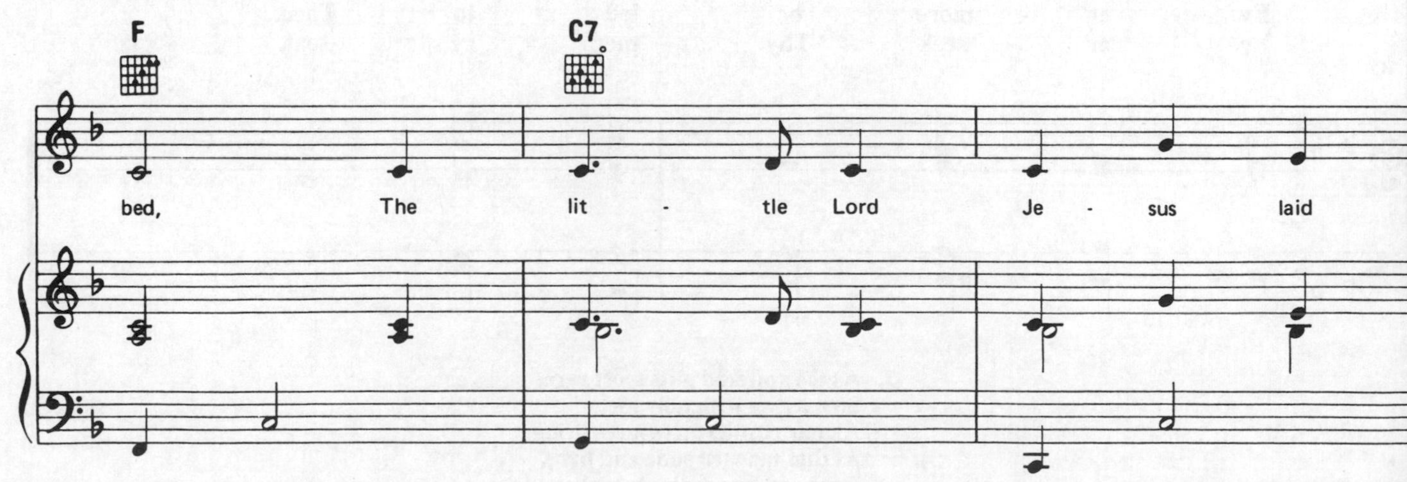
F
C7
bed, The lit - tle Lord Je - sus laid

F
down His sweet head. The stars in the
Bb
F
sky looked down where he lay, The
C7
F
Bb
C7
lit - tle Lord Je - sus, a - sleep on the
F
Bb
hay. The cat - tle are low - ing the ba - by a -

F
C7
wakes, But lit - tle Lord Je - sus, no
F
cry - ing he makes. I love thee, Lord
Bb
F
Je - sus, look down from the sky, And
C7
F
Gm7
F/A
Bb
C7
F
stay by my cra - dle till morn - ing is nigh.

BECAUSE IT'S CHRISTMAS
(For All the Children)

Music by BARRY MANILOW
Lyric by BRUCE SUSSMAN and JACK FELDMAN

Moderately slow
C
Fmaj7
F6
C
p
Fmaj7
F6
C(add9)
C
To-night the stars shine for the
To-night be-longs to all the
mf
Fmaj7
F6
Dm
Gsus
G
chil - dren. and light the way for dreams to
chil - dren. To - night their joy rings through the
C
Am
Am(maj7)
Am7
fly. To-night our love comes wrapped in
air. And so, we send our ten - der

Dm7
F/G
G7
rib - bons.
bless - ings
The world is right and hopes are
to all the chil - dren ev - 'ry
C
Am
high.
where
And from a dark and frost - ed
to see the smiles and hear the
G/F
F
E7sus
E7
win - dow a child ap - pears
laugh - ter; a time to give,
to search the
a time to
Am
1
Dm7
F/G
G
sky be-cause it's Christ - mas, be-cause it's Christ - mas.
share be-cause it's

2
A♭
C/G
Am7
C/D
D
Christ - mas for now_ and for ev - er for all_ of the chil - dren and for the
F/G
G7
C
Fmaj7
F6
chil - dren in us all.
A♭/B♭
Cm/B♭
B♭
A♭/B♭
B♭
E♭
To-night be - longs_ to all the
A♭maj7
A♭6
Fm7
Fm7/B♭
B♭7
E♭(add9)
E♭
chil - dren. To-night_ their joy rings_ through the air.

Cm
Cm(maj7)
Cm7
Fm7
And __ so, we send our ten - der bless - ings
Ab/Bb
Bb
Eb
to all __ the chil - dren __ ev - 'ry - where.
Cm
Bb/Ab
Ab
To see the smiles _ and hear the laugh - ter; a time _ to
G7sus
G7
Cm
Cb
give, a time _ to share be-cause _ it's Christ-mas for now _ and for -

E♭/B♭
Cm7
E♭/F
F
A♭/B♭
B♭
ev - er for all — of the chil - dren and for the chil - dren
A♭/B♭
B♭7♭9
E♭
A♭maj7
A♭6
in us all.
Vocal 1st time only
Fm7
B♭sus
B♭
E♭
Cm
Cm(maj7)
Cm7
Fm7
A♭/B♭
B♭
E♭
A♭/B♭
Repeat and Fade

BABY, IT'S COLD OUTSIDE

from the Motion Picture NEPTUNE'S DAUGHTER

By FRANK LOESSER

Relaxed jazz tempo (played as)
B♭6
G+7
C9
F7#5
B9
Vamp 'til ready
(Patter over vamp)
Female: I
mf
B♭6
Cm7
B♭add9/D
G7#5
real - ly can't stay. ___
sim - ply must go. ___
I've
The
Male: But ba - by, it's cold ___ out - side. ___
But ba - by, it's cold ___ out - side. ___
Cm7
F9
Cm7
F7#9
got to go 'way. ___
an - swer is "No!" ___
This
The
But ba - by, it's cold out - side. ___
But ba - by, it's cold out - side. ___

B♭6 Cm7 B♭/D Gm7 G♭9
eve - ning has been so very - y
wel - come has been so nice and
Been hop - ing that you'd drop in.
How luck - y that you dropped in.
Fm9 B♭9♯11 Fm9 B♭13 E9 E♭maj9 E♭6/9
nice. My moth - er will start to
warm. My sis - ter will be sus -
I'll hold your hands. They're just like ice.
Look out the win - dow at the storm.
E♭maj9 E♭6/9 E♭m7/A♭ A♭9
wor - ry, and Fath - er will be pac - ing the
pi - cious. My broth - er will be there at the
Beau - ti - ful, what's your hur - ry?
Gosh, your lips look de - li - cious. Like

E♭m7/A♭
A♭7
B♭9♯11
A♭13♯11
floor. So real - ly, ha! I'd bet - ter scur -
door. My maid - en aunt's mind is
Lis - ten to the fi - re - place roar.
waves up - on a trop - i - cal shore.
G7♯9
D♭9♯11
C13
C7♭13
Cm7/F
ry! Well, may - be just a half a drink more. My
vi - cious. Well, may - be just a cig - a - rette more. I've
Beau - ti - ful, please don't hur - ry. Put some re - cords on while I pour.
Gosh, your lips are de - li - cious. Nev - er such a bliz - zard be - fore.
B♭6
Cm7
B♭add9/D
G7♯9
neigh - bors might think. Say!
got to get home. (Spoken:) Say, darling,
Ba - by, it's bad out there!
Ba - by, you'd freeze out there.

Cm7
F9
Cm7
F7#9
What's in this drink?
I
can you lend me your comb?
You've
No cabs to be___ had out there.__
It's up to your___ knees out there.__
B♭6
Cm7
B♭add9/D
Gm7
G♭9
Fm9
B♭9#11
wish I knew how___ to___ break the spell.
real-ly been grand,___ but___ don't you see.
Your eyes are like star-light___ now
I'll take your hat.
I thrill when you touch my___ hand.
How can you do
Fm9
B♭13
E9
E♭maj9
D♭9
I ought to say, "No, no, no, sir!"
At
There's bound to be talk to-mor-row.
At
Your hair looks swell.
Mind if I move in
this thing to me?
Think of my life-long

C13
C7♭13
Cm7/F
F7
least I'm gon - na say ___ that I tried. ___ I
least there will be plen - ty im - plied. ___ I
clos - er? What's the sense of hurt - ing my pride?
sor - row if you caught pneu - mo - nia and died. _
B♭6
A♭13#11
G7
real - ly can't stay. Ah, but it's
real - ly can't stay.
Oh ba - by, don't hold out. Ah, but it's
Get o - ver that old doubt.
1
C7
F7♭9
B♭add9
G7#5(♭9)
C7#9(♭13)
F7#9
cold out - side.
cold out - side.

B♭6/9
G7#9
C7#9
F13
C7
I
cold
cold
E♭m7
out
out
B♭9
D7#9
E♭maj9
E7#5(♭9)
Cm7/F
F7
B♭13#11
side.
side.
rit.

THE BELLS OF CHRISTMAS

Music by BARRY MANILOW
Lyric by ADRIENNE ANDERSON

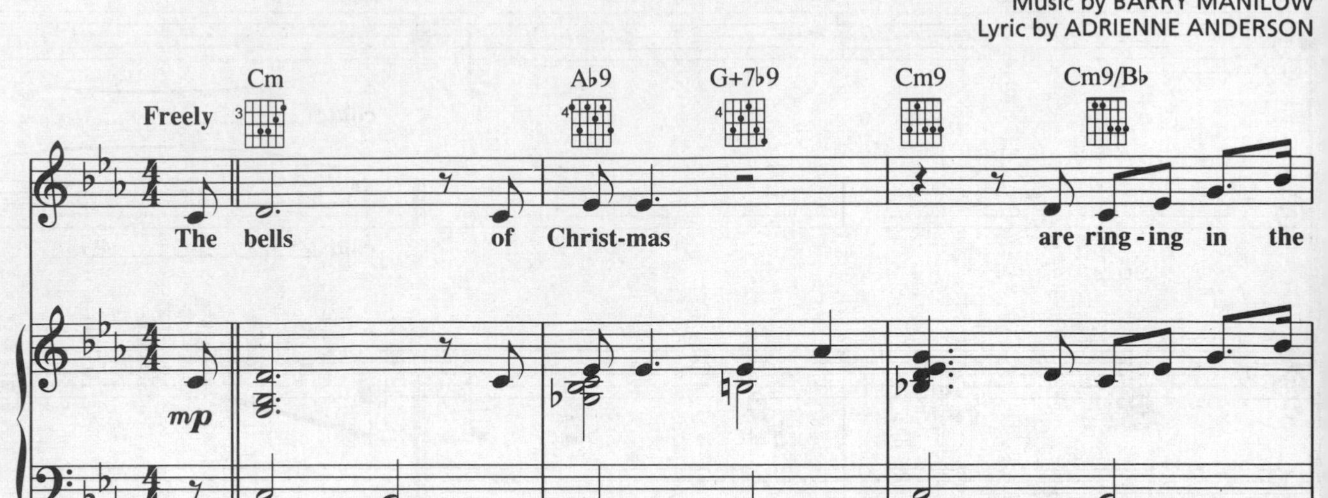
Freely
Cm
A♭9
G+7♭9
Cm9
Cm9/B♭
The bells of Christ-mas are ring-ing in the
mp

F13
F7♭13
Cm9
Fm9
B♭13
night. The chil-dren string their lights up-on the

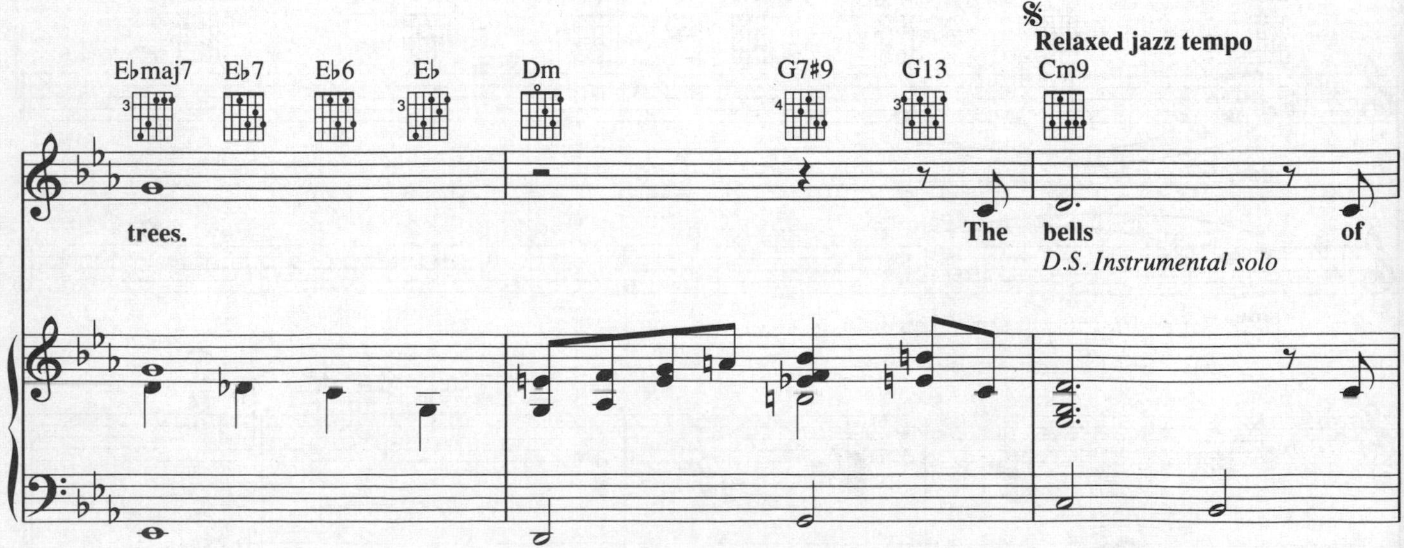
E♭maj7
E♭7
E♭6
E♭
Dm
G7♯9
G13
Relaxed jazz tempo
Cm9
trees. The bells of
D.S. Instrumental solo

A♭9
G7♯5(♭9)
Cm9
Cm9/B♭
Christ - mas,
they sing to me to - night,
F7
F7♯5
Cm9
Cm9/B♭
A♭maj7
D7♭5
D7
bring back thoughts of
you
and
Gmaj7
G7
G6
G
Gm11
me.
Cen - tral Park,
Solo ends
Sun - day walks
C7♯11
C
C9
C7♭9
Fmaj7
F7
slid - ing 'round
in the snow.
watch - ing ships
in the bay.

F6
F
A♭maj7/B♭
And then, af - ter dark,
Mid - night talks. We
B♭13
B♭9
B♭7♭9
E♭maj7
E♭7
E♭6
feel - ing the fire's burn - ing
vowed we'd nev - er let love slip a -
Dm7
G7♭9(♯11)
Cm9
Cm9/B♭
glow.
way.
The bells of
A♭9
G7♯5(♭9)
Cm9
Cm9/B♭
To Coda
Christ - mas, they ring of what could

Am7♭5
Ab9#11
Gm7
Cm7
be. For the bells of Christ - mas, they
Fm7
A♭maj9/B♭
B♭13♭9
E♭
E♭6
ring for you and me.
D.S. al Coda
Dm7
G7#5(♭9)
G7#5(#9)
CODA
Am7♭5
be. For the
A♭9#11
Gm7
Cm7
Am7♭5
A♭9#11
bells of Christ - mas the bells of

Gm7
Cm7
Am7♭5
A♭9♯11
Gm7
Cm7
Christ - mas the bells of Christ - mas they
Fm7
A♭maj7/B♭
B♭13♭9
Moderately, not too fast
E♭
ring for you and me.
rit.
E♭/D
Cm
E♭
D♭
B♭m9
G7♭9
Cm6
rit.

CAROLING, CAROLING

Words by WIHLA HUTSON
Music by ALFRED BURT

With a lilt
G Bm G Bm Am Bm Am7 D7
Car - o - ling, Car - o - ling, now we go; Christ - mas bells are
Car - o - ling, Car - o - ling, thru the town; Christ - mas bells are
Car - o - ling, Car - o - ling, near and far; Christ mas bells are
mf
Gmaj7 Em Bm E6 Bm7 E6 Em7 A7
ring - ing! Car - o - ling, Car - o - ling, thru the snow; Christ - mas bells are
ring - ing! Car - o - ling, Car - o - ling, up and down; Christ - mas bells are
ring - ing! Fol - low - ing, fol - low - ing, yon - der star; Christ - mas bells are
D Am E7 Am A7 D A7 D G Am G Adim
ring - ing! Joy - ous voic - es sweet and clear, Sing the sad of
ring - ing! Mark ye well the song we sing, Glad - some tid - ings
ring - ing! Sing we all this hap - py morn, "Lo, the King of
Em B7 Em C G D7 G C6 G Am7 D Gsus G
heart to cheer. Ding, dong, ding, dong, Christ - mas bells are ring - ing!
now we bring. Ding, dong, ding, dong, Christ - mas bells are ring - ing!
heav'n is born!" Ding, dong, ding, dong, Christ - mas bells are ring - ing!

BRING A TORCH, JEANNETTE, ISABELLA

17th Century French Provençal Carol

Brightly

mf

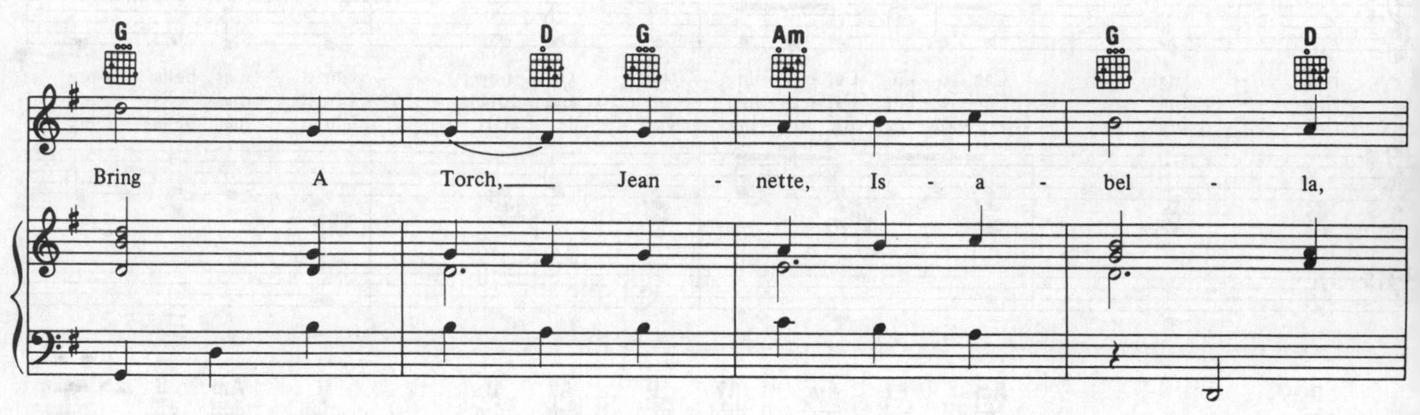
G
D
G
Am
G
D
Bring A Torch, Jean - nette, Is - a - bel - la,

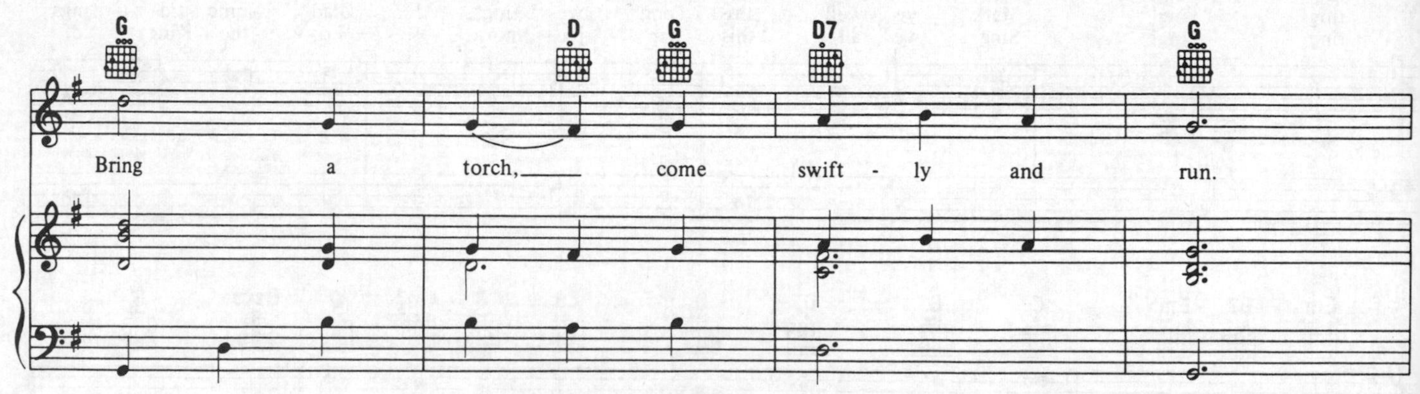
G
D
G
D7
G
Bring a torch, come swift - ly and run.

A7/E
G/D
D
Christ is born, tell the folk of the vil - lage,
C
G
D7/A
G
D7
Em
Je - sus is sleep - ing in His cra - dle, Ah,
D
G
D7
G
D7
Em
ah, Beau - ti - ful is the Moth - er, Ah,
D
G
D7
G
ah, Beau - ti - ful is her Son.

Hasten now, good folk of the village,
Hasten now, the Christ Child to see.
You will find him asleep in a manger,
Quietly come and whisper softly,
Hush, hush, Peacefully now He slumbers,
Hush, hush, Peacefully now He sleeps.

C-H-R-I-S-T-M-A-S

Words by JENNY LOU CARSON
Music by EDDY ARNOLD
Moderato (with expression)
p
C C7 F C G7
When I was but a young - ster Christ - mas meant one thing That I'd be get - ting lots of toys that
C G7 C G7 C
day. I learned a whole lot diff - 'rent when moth - er sat me down And
D7 G7 C
taught me to spell Christ - mas this way. "C" is for the Christ child

F C G7 C
born up - on this day, "H" for her - ald an - gels in the night. "R" means our Re -
F G7 C
deem - er, "I" means Is - ra - el, "S" is for the star that shone so bright.
G7 C D7
"T" is for three wise men, They who trav - eled far, "M," is for the man - ger where He
G7 C F
lay. "A"'s for all He stands for, "S" means shep - herds came And
G7 1 C Dm7 G7 2 C F C
that's why there's a Christ - mas day. day.

CHRISTMAS IS JUST ABOUT HERE

Words and Music by
LOONIS McGLOHON

Joyfully
N.C.
mf
B♭maj7
Bm7♭5
B♭/C
C13
2 fr
Gm7
C7
It's fun hang - ing 'round in the
great fun when Pa - pa will
Am7
Dm
B♭
G/B
C
kitch - en, where ev - 'ry - thing smells so nice; oh,
take us to pick out a Christ - mas tree; Mom

Gm C Am7 Dm7 G7
Ma - ma is bak - ing a fruit - cake with ap - ples, hon - ey and
says to be sure that we choose one that's big and tall - er than
C Gm7 C7 Am7 Dm
spice. The chil - dren are get - ting ex - cit - ed when -
me. It's time to start wrap - ping the pres - ents for
B♭ G/B C Gm C
ev - er grey clouds ap - pear; the al - ma - nac prom - ised a
ev - 'ry - one we hold dear, then hid - ing them back in the
Am7 Dm7 Gm7 Am7 B♭maj7 B♭/C F
snow - fall, and Christ - mas is just a - bout here.
clos - et, 'cause Christ - mas is just a - bout here.

Fm7
B♭7
E♭
3 fr
Cm7
3 fr
Fm7
B♭7
'Tis the sea - son to be jol - ly, ev - 'ry - bod - y feels
Deck the halls with boughs of hol - ly, fill up the can - dy
Gm7
Cm7
3 fr
Gm7
C7
F
C/E
Dm7
young. Deck the halls with boughs of hol - ly and
jar. Light a can - dle in the win - dow and
C/G
G7
Gm7/C
C7
Gm7
C7
let the stock - ings be hung. We'll soon have a vis - it from Saint
hang up the Christ - mas star. I like ev - 'ry - thing a - bout Christ -
Am7
Dm
B♭
G
G7/B
C
Nick, and may - be he'll bring rein - deer. We
mas, the hol - ly and hol - i - day cheer. Let's

To Coda
Gm
C
Fmaj7
D7
Gm7
Am7
B♭maj7
B♭/C
3 fr
nev - er out - grow the warm feel - ing when Christ-mas is just a - bout
hur - ry up and get read - y, 'cause Christ-mas is just a - bout
F
F(add2)
B♭
here.
Ev - 'ry - bod - y
Cm/B♭
Dm7
Cm7
B♭maj7
has a list of things to do.
B♭
Cm/B♭
Dm7
Cm7
Buy a tie for Dad which will look good with

B♭maj7
C
Dm/C
Cmaj9
Dm7/C
blue. Did you mail Aunt Mar - y Lou a Christ - mas
C
Gm7
G13
2 fr
Gm7
card? Tie a rib - bon on the lamp - post out in the
B♭/C
C7
B♭maj7
Am7
Gm7
C13
2 fr
D.S. al Coda
yard. It's
CODA
F
Gm9
3 fr
Fmaj7
N.C.
here.
8va

THE CHRISTMAS SONG
(Chestnuts Roasting on an Open Fire)

Music and Lyric by MEL TORME
and ROBERT WELLS

Sentimentally
Eb6
Bb7
Cm7
Ab
Abm
Eb/Bb
Bdim7
Cm
mf
Fm9
Bb7b9
Eb6
Bb7
Eb6
Bb9
rit.
a tempo
Chest - nuts roast - ing on an o - pen fire,
Eb6
Eb9
Ab
Ab7
G7#5
Cm
Cm/Bb
Abm6
Jack Frost nip - ping at your nose,
yule - tide car - ols be - ing
Eb/Bb
Am7
D7
G
Abm7
Db9
Gbmaj7
Bb7
sung by a choir and folks dressed up like Es - ki - mos. Ev - 'ry - bod - y

Eb6 Bb7 Eb6 Bb9 Eb6 Eb9
knows a tur - key and some mis - tle - toe help to make the sea - son
Ab Ab7 G7#5 Cm Cm/Bb Abm6 Eb/Bb Am7 D7
bright. Ti - ny tots with their eyes all a - glow will
Gm7 C7 Fm7 Bb7 Eb6 Bbm7 Eb9
find it hard to sleep to - night. They know that San - ta's on his
Bbm7 Eb9 Bbm7 Eb9 Abmaj7
way; he's load - ed lots of toys and good - ies on his sleigh, and ev - 'ry

Abm7 Db9 Gbmaj7 Cm7 F7
mother's child is gon-na spy to see if rein-deer real-ly know how to
Bb7sus Bb7 Eb6 Bb7 Eb6 Bb9
fly. And so I'm of-fer-ing this sim-ple phrase to
Eb6 Eb9 Ab Ab7 G7#5 Cm Cm/Bb Abm6
kids from one to nine-ty-two. Al-though it's been said man-y
Eb/Bb Am7 Ab9 Eb/Bb Cm7 Fm7 Bb7b9 Eb6 Fm7/Bb Bb13b9 Eb6
times, man-y ways, "Mer-ry Christ-mas to you." you."
rit. a tempo rit.

CHRISTMAS TIME IS HERE

from A CHARLIE BROWN CHRISTMAS

Words by LEE MENDELSON
Music by VINCE GUARALDI

Slowly
Fmaj9
C13♭9
Fmaj9
C13♭9
mp
With pedal
Fmaj9
E♭13♯11
Fmaj9
Christ - mas time is here, hap - pi - ness and
Snow - flakes in the air, car - ols ev - 'ry -
E♭13♯11
Bm7♭5
B♭m7
Am7
A♭m7
4fr
cheer. Fun for all that chil - dren call their
where. Old - en times and an - cient rhymes of
Gm7
3fr
Gm7♭5/C
Fmaj9
Fmaj9
1
2
fa - v'rite time of year.
love and dreams to share.

Db maj7
Gb13#11
Sleigh-bells in the air,
beau-ty ev - 'ry - where.
Am7
Eb9
D9
D7b9
Gm7
Db9
C13
C13b9
Yule-tide by the fire - side and joy-ful mem - 'ries there.
Fmaj9
Eb13#11
E13#11
Christ-mas time is here,
we'll be draw - ing near.
To Coda
Bm7b5
Bbm7
Ab m7
Bb/C
Oh, that we could al-ways see such spir - it through the year.

E♭13♯11
Fmaj9
E♭13♯11
Bm7♭5
B♭m7
Am7
A♭m7
4 fr
Gm7
3 fr
B♭/C
Fmaj9
E♭13♯11
Fmaj9
E♭13♯11
Bm7♭5
B♭m7
Am7
A♭m7
4 fr
Gm7
3 fr
B♭/C
Fmaj9
D.S. al Coda
CODA
Fmaj9
year.

COVENTRY CAROL

Words by ROBERT CROO
Traditional English Melody

Tenderly
Gm D Gm F Gm D Gm D Gm
1. Lul - lay, thou lit - tle ti - ny child by by, lul -
2. O sis - ters too, how may we do, for to pre -
mp
Cm D7 Gm Bb F Bb F Bb
ly lul - lay. Lul - lay, thou lit - tle
serve this day. This poor young - ling for
Cm D Gm D Eb Cm D G
ti - ny child. By by, lul - ly, lul - lay.
whom we sing. By by, lul - ly, lul - lay.

3. Herod the king,
In his raging,
Charged he hath this day.
His men of might,
In his own sight,
All young children to slay.

4. That woe is me,
Poor child for thee!
And ever morn and day,
For thy parting
Neither say nor sing
By by, lully lullay!

THE CHRISTMAS WALTZ

Words by SAMMY CAHN
Music by JULE STYNE

Moderately, with expression
mf
rall.
F
D7sus
D7
Gm7
C7
F
Frost - ed win - dow panes, can - dles gleam - ing in - side, Paint - ed can - dy canes
a tempo
D7-9
Gm
C7-9
F
Gm7
on the tree; San - ta's on his way, he's filled his
C7-9
Fmaj7
Dm7
G9
G7-5
C7
C7+5
F
sleigh with things, Things for you and for me. It's that time of year,

D7sus D7 Gm7 C7 F D7-9 Gm

When the world falls in love, Ev'ry song you hear seems to say:

C7-9 F Gm7 C9 Am7-5

"Mer - ry Christ - mas, May your New Year dreams come true."

D7 D7+5 D7 G9 C9 C7 F D7 G7

And this song of mine, in three - quar - ter time, Wish - es you and yours

Cm7 C7 F Dm Gm7 C9 F

the same thing too.

poco rall.

COLD DECEMBER NIGHTS

Words and Music by MICHAEL McCARY
and SHAWN STOCKMAN

Moderately slow
Cmaj9
Fmaj7
mf
With pedal
Am9
Gsus2/B
C
(2nd time only) So cold,
Fmaj7
E7
N.C.
so cold. Oh.
Am9
Gsus2/B
C
Cold De - cem - ber nights like this makes me
the stars shine bright as the night air, and the

Fmaj7
Am9
Gsus2/B
real - ly ___ scared. You're not real - ly ___ there
thought of you not be - ing here makes me shed a ___ tear.
C
Fmaj7
E7/G#
and my tree is real - ly bare. ___ An - oth - er lone -
And yet mat - ters re - main un - clear 'bout why ___ you're gone, ___
Am9
Gsus2/B
C
Fmaj7
- ly night, ___ no gifts, no toys ___ un - der - neath ___ my ___ tree. ___
___ or if you'll ev - er re - turn ___ to this bro - ken heart. ___
Am9
Gsus2/B
C
___ Can this real - ly ___ be? ___ I'm sing - ing
Life is so torn ___ a - part ___ and God

Fmaj7
E7
N.C.
Christ - mas car - ols and there's no Christ - mas for
knows, God knows where I need to start re -
Am9
Gsus2/B
C
Why aren't you next
me?
build - ing.
Fmaj7
to me
Am9
Gsus2/B
cel - e - brat - ing Christ - mas?
C
Fmaj7
Why can't you see what hurts so bad?
Whoa.

Am9
Gsus2/B
C
Fmaj7
How can you go with - out pay - ing mind
to my sor - row
Am
Gsus2/B
C
You can't i - mag - ine how, how I feel.
on this cold
Fmaj7
E13♭9
De - cem - ber night?
1
N.C.
2
N.C.
Ooh.
Oh.

Cmaj9
Fmaj7
Am9
Gsus2/B
C
Fmaj7
E7
N.C.
Cmaj9
Fmaj7
Why aren't _ you next __ to me ________ cel - e - brat - ing

Am9
Gsus2/B
C
Fmaj7
Christ - mas?
Why can't you see what hurts so bad?
Cmaj9
How can you go
Fmaj7
with - out paying mind to my sor - row?
Am9
Gsus2/B
You can't i - mag - ine how, how I feel.
C
Fmaj7
E7add13
on this cold De - cem - ber night?
Repeat and Fade

DECK THE HALL

Traditional Welsh Carol

Gaily
F
C7
Deck the hall with
See the blaz - ing
Fast a - way the
f
mf

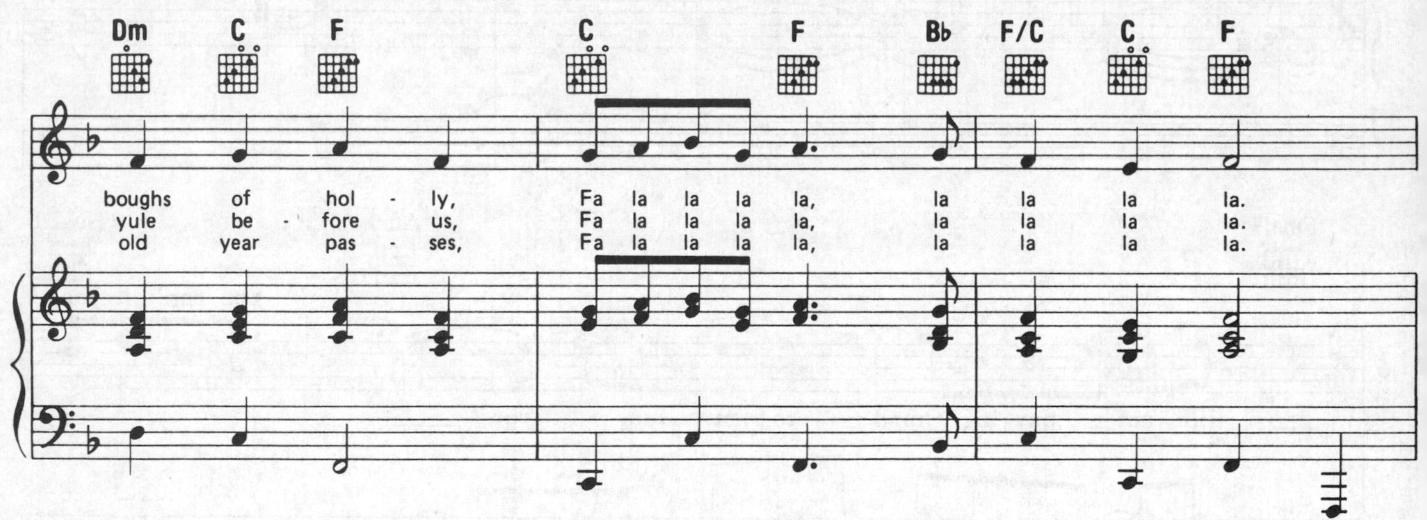
Dm
C
F
C
F
B♭
F/C
C
F
boughs of hol - ly, Fa la la la la, la la la la.
yule be - fore us, Fa la la la la, la la la la.
old year pas - ses, Fa la la la la, la la la la.

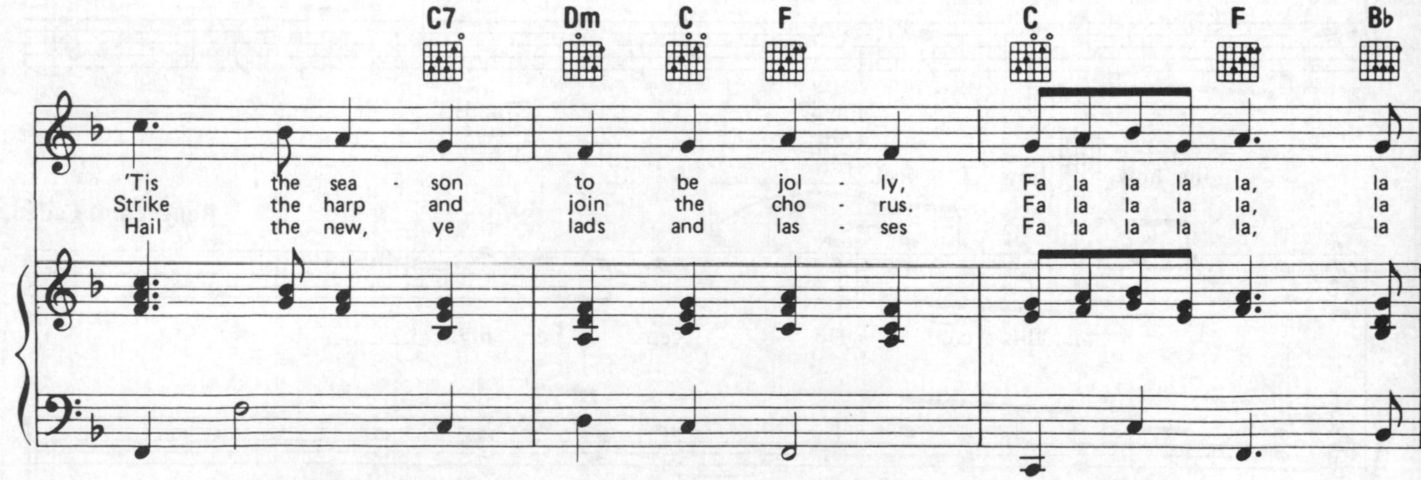
C7
Dm
C
F
C
F
B♭
'Tis the sea - son to be jol - ly, Fa la la la la, la
Strike the harp and join the cho - rus. Fa la la la la, la
Hail the new, ye lads and las - ses Fa la la la la, la

F/C C F C F C
la la la. Don we now our gay ap - par - el,
la la la. Fol - low me in mer - ry mea - sure,
la la la. Sing we joy - ous, all to - geth - er
Am Dm C/G G7 C F C7
Fa la la la la la la la la. Troll the an - cient
Fa la la la la la la la la. While I tell of
Fa la la la la la la la la. Heed - less of the
Dm C F Bb F/A Bb F/C C7 F
Yule - tide car - ol. Fa la la la la, la la la la.
Yule - tide treas - ure. Fa la la la la, la la la la.
wind and weath - er. Fa la la la la, la la la la.

DING DONG! MERRILY ON HIGH!

French Carol

Moderately
E♭
B♭/D
Cm7
F7
B♭
B♭7/D
E♭
C7
mf
Ding dong! Mer - ri - ly on
E'en so here be - low, be -
F7
E♭
C9
F7
B♭
high in heav'n the bells are ring - ing.
low, let stee - ple bells be swung - en,
B♭7/D
E♭
C7
F7
E♭
C9
F7
Ding dong! Ver - i - ly the sky is riv'n with an - gel
And i - o, i - o, i - o, by priest and peo - ple

B♭
Dm
Gm7
Cm7
F7
sing - ing.
sung - en.
Glo - - - - - - - ri - a, Ho - san - na in ex - cel - sis!
Gm
Am7♭5
D7
B♭/D
E♭
E♭maj7
C7

3. Pray you, dutifully prime your matin chime, ye ringers;
May you beautiful rime your evetime song, ye singers.

DO THEY KNOW IT'S CHRISTMAS?

Words and Music by M. URE and B. GELDOF

Medium Rock
C
mf
F
F/G
C
It's Christ - mas - time, there's no need to be a - fraid.
F
F/G
G
C
At Christ - mas - time, we let in light and we ban - ish shade.
F
G
C
And in our world of plen - ty we can spread a smile of joy

F
Dm
G6
C
Throw your arms a - round the world at Christ - mas - time.
F
G
C
But say a prayer, to pray for the oth - er ones
F
G
C
at Christ - mas - time. It's hard, but when you're hav - ing fun
F
G
C
there's a world out - side your win - dow, and it's a world of dread and fear

F
Dm7
G
C
— where the on - ly wa - ter flow - ing is — the bit - ter sting of
F
Dm7
G
C
tears. And the Christ - mas bells — that ring — there — are the clang - ing chimes of doom. —
F
Dm7
G
C
— Well, to - night thank God it's them — in - stead of you.
Csus
C
F
G
C
And there won't be snow — in Af - ri - ca — this Christ - mas - time, —

F
G
C
the great-est gift_ they'll get this year_ is life.___ Oh._
Dm/C
C
F
G
C
Where noth-ing ev-er grows,__ no rain or riv-ers flow,_
F
Dm7
F/G
C
do they know it's Christ-mas-time at_ all?
F
C
Am
G
Am
G
Here's to you, raise a glass for ev'-ry-one; here's to them un-der-neath that burn-ing sun.

F
F/G
C
F
C/E
F
C/E
Do they know it's Christ-mas-time at all?
Dm7
Dm7/G
C
F
C/E
F
C/E
Dm7
Dm7/G
Feed the world.
C
F
C/E
F
Am/E
Dm7
Dm7/G
Feed the world, let them know it's Christ - mas - time a -
C
F
C/E
Feed the world,
F
Am/E
Dm7
Dm7/G
Repeat and Fade
gain. let them know it's Christ - mas - time a -

EMMANUEL

Words and Music by
MICHAEL W. SMITH

Steadily
N.C.
mf
F
B♭m/F
Em - man - u - el, Em -
man - u - el.
B♭
Am7
Dm
Won - der - ful Coun - sel - or,
C
Lord of life, Lord of all,
He's the

B♭
Am7
Dm
E♭
3fr
To Coda
Prince of Peace, Might - y God, Ho - ly One, Em -
E♭maj7
F/E♭
E♭
F/E♭
Dm
B♭
1
Csus
C
man - u - el, Em - man - u -
F
2
Csus(add2)
C
D♭
el. Em- Em - man - u - el.
C7sus
B♭m7
C7sus
C
F
D.S. al Coda
Em -
mp

CODA
E♭
3fr
D7
Gm
3fr
F/A
B♭
Em - man - u - el,
Em - man - u -
el!
C(add4)
B♭
ff
sub. mp
slightly detached
C(add4)
Gm7
3fr
C(add4)/G
building
Gm7
3fr
C7sus
Em -

B♭m/F
F
man - u - el, Em -
mp
B♭m/F
1
F
2
F
man - u - el. Em - el.
B♭
Am7
Dm
Won-der-ful Coun-sel - or,
Lord of life, Lord of all,
f
C
B♭
Am7
Dm
He's the Prince of Peace, Might - y God,

E♭
E♭maj7
F/E♭
E♭
F/E♭
3fr
Ho - ly One,
Em - man - u -
Dm
B♭
Csus
C
Play 4 times
el,
Em - man - u -
B♭m/F
F
B♭m/F
el.
Em - man - u -
F
B♭m/E♭
F
Play 3 times
el,
Em - man - u - el.
slight rit.

FELIZ NAVIDAD

Music and Lyrics by
JOSE FELICIANO

Moderately
Em7
A7
D
G
mf
D
N.C.
Em7
A7
Fe - liz Na - vi - dad.
Fe - liz Na - vi -
D
Em6
dad.
Fe - liz Na - vi - dad.
Pros - pe - ro

A7
1
D
N.C.
a - ño y fe - li - ci - dad.
Fe - liz Na - vi -
2
D
To next strain
3
D
I want to wish you a
Fine
G
A7
Mer - ry Christ - mas,
with lots of pres - ents to
D
G
make you hap - py.
I want to wish you a Mer - ry Christ - mas from the

A7
Em7
A7
D
G
D
bot - tom of my heart.
I want to wish you a
G
A7
D
Mer - ry Christ - mas, with mis - tle - toe and lots of cheer.
G
With lots of laugh - ter through - out the years from the
A7
Em7
A7
D
G
D
N.C.
D.S. al Fine
bot - tom of my heart.
Fe - liz Na - vi -

FROSTY THE SNOW MAN

Words and Music by STEVE NELSON
and JACK ROLLINS

Moderately
F
F#dim7
C/G
A7
Dm7
G7
C6
mf
C
C7
F
F#dim7
Fros - ty the Snow Man was a jol - ly, hap - py soul
Fros - ty the Snow Man knew the sun was hot that day,
C/G
F
F#dim7
C/G
A7
with a corn - cob pipe and a but - ton nose and two
so he said, "Let's run and we'll have some fun now be -
Dm7
G7
C
G7
C
C7
eyes made out of coal. Fros - ty the Snow Man is a
fore I melt a - way." Down to the vil - lage with a

F F#dim7 C/G F F#dim7
fair - y tale, they say; he was made of snow but the
broom - stick in his hand, run - ning here and there all a -
C/G A Dm7 G7 C C7
chil - dren know how he came to life one day. There
round the square say - in', "Catch me if you can." He
F F#dim7 C/G A7 Dm7 G7 C
must have been some mag - ic in that old silk hat they found, for
led them down the streets of town right to the traf - fic cop, and he
G A♭dim7 Am7 D9 G G7#5
4fr
when they placed it on his head he be - gan to dance a - round. Oh,
on - ly paused a mo - ment when he heard him hol - ler, "Stop!" For

C
C7
F
F#dim7
C/G
Fros - ty the Snow Man was a - live as he could be, and the
Fros - ty the Snow Man had to hur - ry on his way, but he
F
F#dim7
C/G
A
Dm7
G7
C
chil - dren say he could laugh and play just the same as you and me.
waved good - bye say - in', "Don't you cry, I'll be back a - gain some - day."
G7
Thump-et - y thump thump, thump-et - y thump thump, look at Fros - ty go.
lightly
C
Thump-et - y thump thump, thump-et - y thump thump, o - ver the hills of snow.

THE FIRST NOEL

17th Century English Carol
Music from *W. Sandys' Christmas Carols*

Moderately slow
A7
The
D Bm A A7 D G D A7 D A7
first No - ël, the an - gel did say, Was to cer - tain poor
D G A7 D A7 D A7 D Bm A A7
shep - herds in fields as they lay; In fields where they lay

D
G
D
A7
D
A7
D
G
A7
D
A7
keep - ing their sheep, On a cold win - ter's night that was so
Refrain
D
A7
D
Bm
F♯m
D
G
D
A
deep. No - ël, No - ël, No - ël, No - ël,
Bm
D
G
D
A7
D
A7
D
Born is the King of Is - ra - el.

Additional Lyrics

2. They looked up and saw a star
Shining in the East, beyond them far.
And to the earth it gave great light
And so it continued both day and night.
Refrain

3. And by the light of that same star,
Three wise men came from country far;
To seek for a King was their intent,
And to follow the star wherever it went.
Refrain

4. This star drew nigh to the northwest,
O'er Bethlehem it took its rest;
And there it did both stop and stay,
Right over the place where Jesus lay.
Refrain

5. Then entered in those wise men three,
Full reverently upon their knee;
And offered there in His presence,
Their gold, and myrrh, and frankincense.
Refrain

THE FRIENDLY BEASTS

Traditional English Carol

Moderately
F
C7
Je - sus our broth - er, kind and
mp
F
B♭
good Was hum - bly born in a
C7
F
sta - ble rude, And the friend - ly

B♭/F
F
C7
F
beasts a - round Him stood,
B♭
F
Dm
Gm/B♭
C7
F
Je - sus our broth - er, kind and good.

Additional Lyrics

2. "I," said the donkey, shaggy and brown,
"I carried His mother up hill and down;
I carried her safely to Bethlehem town."
"I," said the donkey, shaggy and brown.

3. "I," said the cow all white and red,
"I gave Him my manger for His bed;
I gave Him my hay to pillow His head."
"I," said the cow all white and red.

4. "I," said the sheep with curly horn,
"I gave Him my wool for His blanket warm;
He wore my coat on Christmas morn."
"I," said the sheep with curly horn.

5. "I," said the dove from the rafters high,
"I cooed Him to sleep so He would not cry;
We cooed Him to sleep, my mate and I."
"I," said the dove from the rafters high.

6. Thus every beast by some good spell,
In the stable dark was glad to tell
Of the gift he gave Emanuel,
The gift he gave Emanuel.

FUM, FUM, FUM

Traditional Catalonian Carol

Joyfully

f

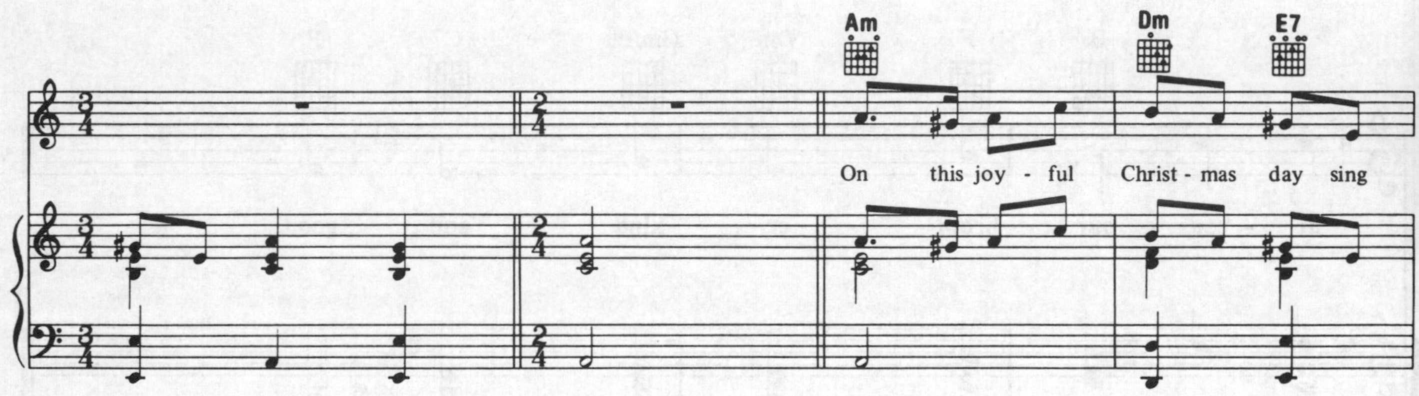
Am
Dm
E7
On this joy - ful Christ - mas day sing

Am
E7
Am
Dm
E7
Fum, Fum, Fum. On this joy - ful Christ - mas day sing

Am E7 Am C Fdim/C C
Fum, Fum, Fum. For a bless - ed Babe was born up - on this
Fdim/C C F Dm
day at break of morn. In a man - ger poor and
E7 Am E Am Dm E7 Am E7
low - ly lay the Son of God most ho - ly, Fum, Fum,
Am Dm E7 Am E7
Fum. Thanks to God for hol - i - days, sing Fum, Fum,

Am
Dm
E7
Am
E7
Fum. Thanks to God for hol - i - days, sing Fum, Fum,
Am
C
Fdim/C
C
Cmaj7
C
Fdim/C
Fum. Now we all our voic - es raise, and sing a song of grate - ful
C
F
Dm
E7
Am
E
praise, Cel - e - brate in song and stor - y, all the
Am
Dm
E7
Am
E7
Am
won - ders of his glo - ry, Fum, Fum, Fum.

THE GIFT

Words and Music by TOM DOUGLAS
and JIM BRICKMAN

Slow Ballad
B♭(add9)
F(add4)/A
Gm
F6
mf
E♭(add9)
Fsus
F7sus
F7
Female: Hoo.
B♭(add9)
F/A
Gm
B♭/F
Win-ter snow is fall - ing down, chil-dren laugh-ing all a - round,
E♭(add9)
B♭/D
Cm7
Fsus
F
lights are turn-ing on, like a fair - y tale come true.

B♭
F/A
Gm
3fr
B♭/F
Sit-ting by the fire we made, you're the an-swer when I prayed
E♭
3fr
B♭/D
Cm7
3fr
F7sus
I would find some - one and ba-by, I found you.
F
B♭/D
E♭
3fr
Fsus
All I want is to hold you for - ev-er.
F
B♭/D
E♭
3fr
Fsus
All I need is you more ev-'ry day.

F
B♭/D
D7
You saved my heart from be-ing
Gm
Gm/F
Em7♭5
Cm7
B♭/D
bro-ken a-part. You gave your love a-way and I'm thank-ful
F7sus
B♭
F(add4)/A
ev-'ry day for the gift.
Gm
F6
E♭(add9)

F
C/E
Dm
F/C
Male: Watch-ing as you soft - ly sleep, what I'd give if I could keep
B♭(add9)
6fr
F/A
Gm
3 fr
C
just this mo - ment, if on - ly time stood still.
3
F
C/E
Dm
F/C
But the col-ors fade a - way and the years will make us grey,
B♭
F/A
Gm
3fr
C7sus
but, ba - by, in my eyes, you'll still be beau - ti - ful.

C
F/A
B♭
Csus
3 fr
Both: All I want is to hold you for - ev - er.
All I need is you more ev - 'ry day.
A7
Dm
Dm/C
To Coda
Male: You saved my heart from be-ing bro-ken a - part.
a - part.
Bm7♭5
Gm7
C7sus
Female: You gave your love a-way
Male: and I'm thank-ful ev-'ry day

F
B♭
Both: for the gift.
C
Dm
F/A
B♭(add9)
6fr
F/A
Gm7
3fr
Csus
3fr
C
B♭/D
C/E
F
B♭
Gm7
3fr
F/A
Csus
3fr
C
D.S. al Coda
Both: All I want

CODA
Bm7♭5
Gm7
3 fr
Female: You gave your love a - way.
F/A
B♭
C/D
Dm
Gm7
3 fr
Male: I can't find the words to say Female: that I'm thank - ful ev - 'ry day
rit.
Csus
3 fr
F
C(add4)/E
Dm
Both: for the gift.
a tempo
C6
B♭(add9)
6 fr
Csus
3 fr
F(add9)
Female: Ooh, ah. Male: Ah, ooh, ooh.
rit.

GO, TELL IT ON THE MOUNTAIN

African-American Spiritual
Verses by JOHN W. WORK, JR.

Moderate Swing (played as)
G
C
G/B
Am7
mf
Em7
D7
Go tell it on the moun - tain,
O - ver the hills and ev - 'ry - where;
Go tell it on the

G/B
Em
Cm/E♭
G/D
D7
G
Fine
moun - tain, That Je - sus Christ _ is born.
G
G6
Gmaj7
G7
C6
Cm6/E♭
When I was a seek - er, I sought both night and
He made me a watch - man up - on the cit - y
G
Am7
G
G6
Gmaj7
G7
day; I asked the Lord to help me, And
wall; And if I am a Christ - ian, I
Em7
A7
D7sus
D7
D7sus
D7
D.S. al Fine
He showed me the way.
am the least of all.

GOD REST YE MERRY, GENTLEMEN

19th Century English Carol

Moderately
F/A
C7
F
B♭
F
C7
Dm/A
A
mf
Dm
Dm
A
Dm
Am
B♭
F
God rest ye mer - ry, gen - tle - men, Let
Beth - le - hem, in Jew - ry This
B♭
A
Dm
Gm
A
Dm
A
noth - ing you dis - may, For Je - sus Christ our
bless - ed babe was born, And laid with - in a
Dm
Am
B♭
F
B♭
A
Dm
Gm
A
D
Sav - ior was born up - on this day, To
man - ger, Up - on this bless - ed morn; To

Gm
C
F
B♭
F7
B♭
F
A7
Dm
G
C
F
save us all from Sa - tan's power when we were gone a -
which His moth - er Ma - ry did noth - ing take in
C
Dm
C
F
B♭
F
C7
Dm
A
stray.
scorn.
O tid - ings of com - fort and
Dm
G7
C
C7
Dm
C7
F
B♭
joy, com - fort and joy; O tid - ings of
F
C7
Dm
A
1
Dm
2
Dm
com - fort and joy! In joy!

GOOD KING WENCESLAS

Words by JOHN M. NEALE
Music from Piae Cantiones

With spirit

mf

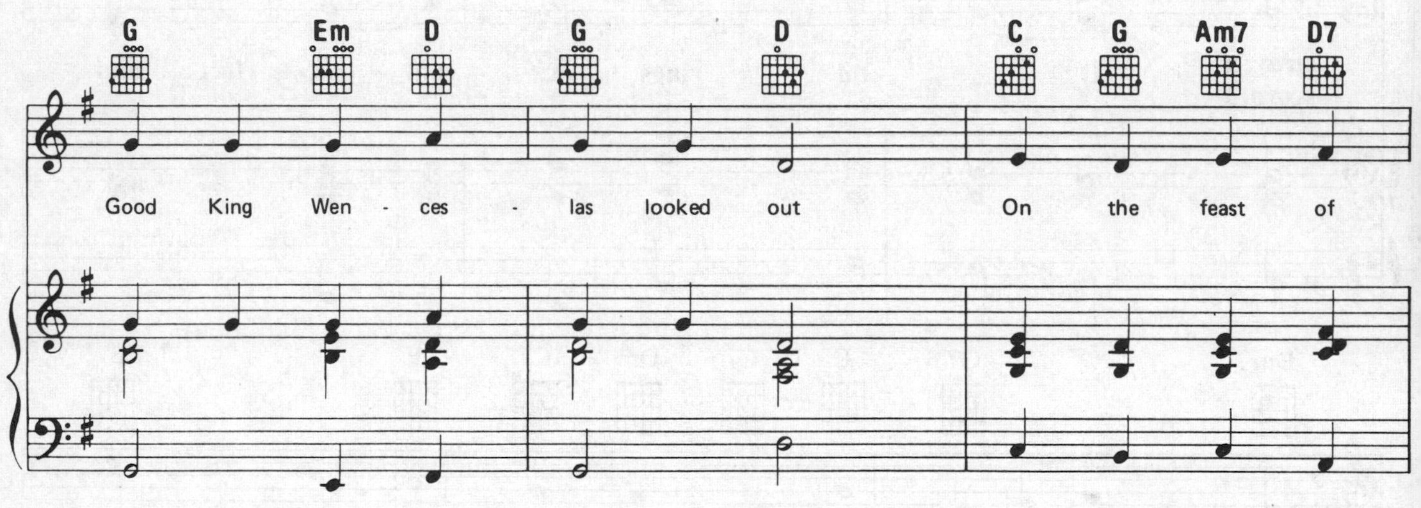
G Em D G D C G Am7 D7
Good King Wen - ces - las looked out On the feast of

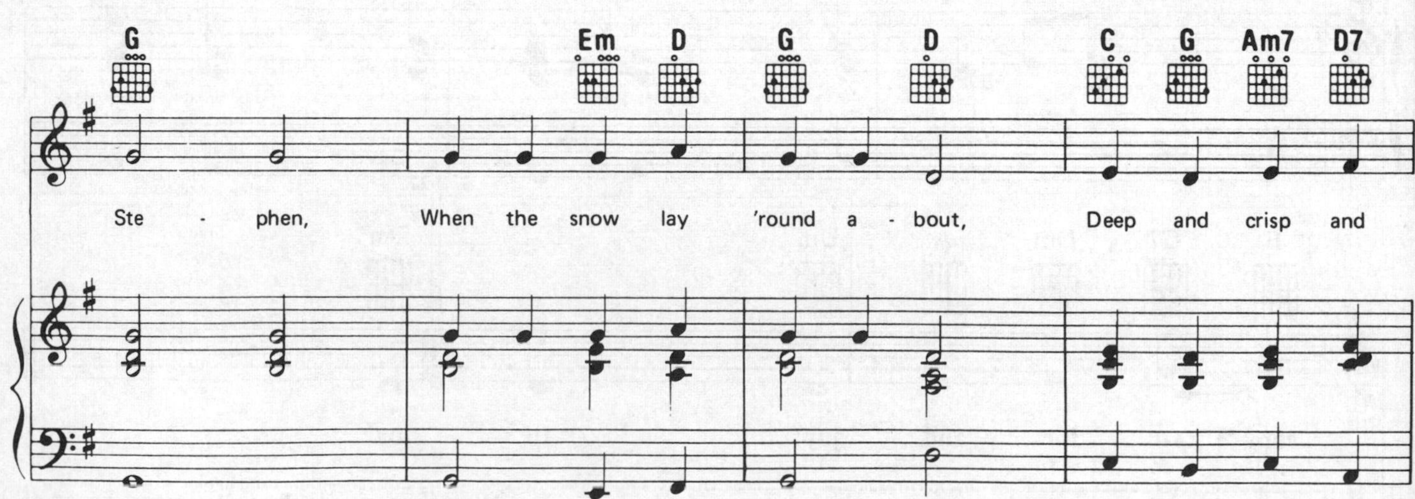
G Em D G D C G Am7 D7
Ste - phen, When the snow lay 'round a - bout, Deep and crisp and

G
Am
G
D7
G
D7
Em
e - ven. Bright - ly shone the moon that night,
C
G
Am7
D7
G
Am7
B7
Though the frost was cru - el. When a poor man
Em
D7
G
Am
G
D
Em
C
G
came in sight, Gath - 'ring win - ter fu - el.

2.
"Hither page, and stand by me,
If thou know'st it, telling,
Yonder peasant, who is he?
Where and what his dwelling?"
"Sire, he lives a good league hence,
Underneath the mountain;
Right against the forest fence,
By Saint Agnes' fountain."

3.
"Bring me flesh, and bring me wine,
Bring me pine-logs hither;
Thou and I will see him dine,
When we bear them thither."
Page and monarch forth they went,
Forth they went together;
Through the rude winds wild lament:
And the bitter weather.

4.
"Sire, the night is darker now,
And the wind blows stronger;
Fails my heart, I know not how,
I can go not longer."
"Mark my footsteps, my good page,
Tread thou in them boldly:
Thou shalt find the winter's rage
Freeze thy blood less coldly."

5.
In his master's steps he trod,
Where the snow lay dinted;
Heat was in the very sod
Which the saint had printed.
Therefore, Christain men, be sure,
Wealth or rank possessing,
Ye who now will bless the poor,
Shall yourselves find blessing.

GRANDMA GOT RUN OVER BY A REINDEER

Words and Music by
RANDY BROOKS

Moderately bright
Em
E
E
mf
Grand-ma got run o - ver by a

A
rein-deer
walk-ing home from our house Christ-mas Eve.

E
B
To Coda
You can say there's no such thing as San - ta,
but as for me and Grand-pa, we be -

E
D
A
E
B
lieve.
1. She'd been drink - ing too much egg - nog
2., 3. (See additional lyrics)
E
E7
and we begged her not to go,
but she for - got her med - i -
A
B
E
ca - tion,
and she stag - gered out the door in - to the snow.
C#m
4fr
G#m
4fr
B7
When we found her Christ - mas morn - ing
at the scene of the at -

E
E7
A
tack,
she had hoof-prints on her fore-head,
and in -
B
1, 2
E
3
E
D.S. al Coda
crim - i - nat - ing Claus marks on her back.
back?
CODA
E
C#
F#
lieve.
Grand - ma got run o - ver by a
B
rein-deer
walk-ing home from our house Christ-mas Eve.

F#
C#
You can say there's no such thing as San - ta,
but as for me and Grand-pa, we be -
F#
C#
F#
lieve.

Additional Lyrics

2. Now we're all so proud of Grandpa,
He's been taking this so well.
See him in there watching football,
Drinking beer and playing cards with Cousin Mel.
It's not Christmas without Grandma.
All the family's dressed in black,
And we just can't help but wonder:
Should we open up her gifts or send them back?
Chorus

3. Now the goose is on the table,
And the pudding made of fig,
And the blue and silver candles,
That would just have matched the hair in Grandma's wig.
I've warned all my friends and neighbors,
Better watch out for yourselves.
They should never give a license
To a man who drives a sleigh and plays with elves.
Chorus

GRANDPA'S GONNA SUE THE PANTS OFFA SANTA

Words and Music by RITA ABRAMS, ELMO SHROPSHIRE and JON GAUGER

Moderately
Cm
Ab/C
F/A
Ab6
G7
3fr
mf
No
Cm
Ab/C
F/C
Ab/C
Cm
Ab/C
doubt you can re-mem-ber Grand-ma's pass-ing, that trag-ic, mourn-ful tale so of-ten
day while griev-ing Grand-pa watched the T V, he heard some ad-ver-tis-ing law-yers
Dm7b5
G7
Dm7b5
G7#5
G7
sung. The prime sus-pect is one of San-ta's rein-deer, in the
swear they'd win a mul-ti-mil-lion dol-lar set-tle-ment and

Dm7♭5
G7
1
Cm
3fr
2 Lively
C
world's most fa-mous case of hit-and-run. One
make his loss much eas-i-er to bear.
Grand-pa's gon-na sue the pants off a San-ta,
G7
that's what Grand-pa's gon-na do.
Grand-pa's gon-na sue the pants
C
off a San-ta 'cause Grand-ma would have want-ed him to.

Grand-pa's gon - na sue the pants off - a San - ta, he
knows the law is
thinks the law is
thought the law was
on his side.
G7
To Coda
Grand-pa's gon - na sue the pants off - a San - ta,
San - ta's go - in' for a ride.
Cm
A♭/C
3fr
F/C
Yes - ter - day the judge ar - raigned the
Now San - ta and the rein - deer wait the

F/C
Ab/C
Cm
Ab/C
Dm7b5
G7
rein - deer, Ru - dolph was the first to take the stand. They
ver - dict de - liv - ered by a jur - y of their peers:
Dm7b5
G7#5
G7
Dm7b5
G7
asked him for the truth a - bout ol' San - ta, Ru - dy said he's just a fat and jol - ly
six fat men with long and flow - ing whis - kers and half a doz - en pok - er - faced rein -
Cm
Ab/C
F/C
Ab/C
man. (Spoken:) Now San - ta is be - fore the pro - se - cu - tion; he
dee. Now Grand - pa gets a T. V. for his suf - f'ring and
Cm
Ab/C
Dm7b5
G7
Dm7b5
looks a lit - tle thin - ner on the stand. (Sung:) And if they take a - way his fly - ing
San - ta is de - clar - ing bank - rupt - cy. (Spoken:) But lis - ten close - ly and you'll hear the

G7#5
G7
Dm7♭5
G7
1
C
li - cense,
there won't be an - y Christ-mas in the land.
law-yers
(Sung:) sing-ing "Jin-gle Bells" as they col-lect their
2
C
D.S. al Coda
CODA
G7
fees.
San - ta's go - in' for a ride.
C
G7
C
And Grand-pa's rid - ing by his side
'cause the
G7
C
C6
law - yers took them for a ride.

THE GREATEST GIFT OF ALL

Words and Music by
JOHN JARVIS

Moderately Slow
D
D/C
G/B
C
G/D
D7
G
C/G
mf
D/G
C/G
G
D/F#
G
Dawn is slow - ly break - ing,
C
G
D/F#
our friends have all gone home.
You and I are
Em
A7
D
wait - ing for San - ta Claus to come.

Copyright © 1984 Sony/ATV Songs LLC
All Rights Administered by Sony/ATV Music Publishing, 8 Music Square West, Nashville, TN 37203
International Copyright Secured All Rights Reserved

G
D/F#
G
G7
C
There's a pres - ent by the tree, stock-ings on the
G
D
D/C
G/B
C
wall. Know-ing you're in love with me is the
G/D
D
G
C/G
G
G7
great - est gift of all.
C
G/B
C
C7
F
The fire is slow - ly fad - ing, chill is in the

C
G/B
Am
air.
All the gifts are wait - ing
D7
G
F/A
G/B
C
G/B
for chil-dren ev' - ry - where.
Through the win - dow
C
C7
F
C
I can see
snow be-gin to fall.
G
G/F
C/E
F
C/G
G
Know-ing you're in love with me is the great - est gift of

C
A7
G/B
A7/C#
D
A/C#
all.
Just be - fore I
D
G
D
go to sleep
I hear a church bell ring.
A/C#
Bm
Bm7
E7
Mer - ry Christ - mas ev' - ry - one
is the song it
A
G/B
A7/C#
D
A/C#
D
sings.
So I say a si - lent prayer

G
D
A7
A7/G
for crea - tures great and small.
Peace on earth good
D7/F#
G
D/A
A7
D
will to men is the great - est gift of all.
A7
A7/G
D7/F#
G
D/A
A
Peace on earth good will to men is the great - est gift
D
G
Em/A
D
of all.
rit.

GREENWILLOW CHRISTMAS
from GREENWILLOW

By FRANK LOESSER

Peacefully
Am
G
Am
Am7
Three wise men fol - lowed a
long a - go in
p
D/A
B♭
Am
G
Am
star one night to where glad bells were peal - ing,
Beth - le - hem yet ev - er live the glo - ry,
G/A
Am
Am7
D/A
B♭
and soon be - held the Ho - ly Child and
and hearts all glow and voic - es rise a -

Am
G
Am
D7sus
D7
all the shep - herds kneel - ing.
ca - rol - ing the sto - ry.
Come
cresc.
mf
G
Dm7
G
Dm7
G
Dm7
see the star, come hear the
G
Dm7
G
Dm7
G
Dm7
bells. Come learn the tale this
G
F
E7sus
E7
E7♭9
Am
Em7
night for - ev - er tells. Come one and

Am
Em7
Am
Em7
F
D
G
F
all from far and wide. Come know the
Eb
G/D
Eb7/Db
G/D
Eb
G/D
G
F
joy, the joy, the joy. Come know the
Eb
G/D
1
Ebmaj7
F
G
Am
G
joy of Christ - mas - tide.
p
2
Ebmaj7
F
G
'Twas Christ - mas - tide.
poco rit.

GROWN-UP CHRISTMAS LIST

Words and Music by DAVID FOSTER
and LINDA THOMPSON-JENNER

Moderately slow
Gm Dm7 E♭ Cm F F/A B♭sus B♭ F/A Gm F6 C/E
mp
With pedal
F(add9) B♭ F Gm
Do you re-mem-ber me? I
Dm7 E♭(add2) E♭ B♭/D Cm7
sat up-on your knee. I wrote to you with child-hood fan-ta-
F7sus F7 B♭ F Gm Dm7 E♭(add2)
sies. Well, I'm all grown up now, and still need help some-how. I'm
chil-dren we be-lieved the grand-est sight to see was

E♭
B♭/D
Cm7
Fsus
F
B♭
F
Gm
not a child _ but my heart still can dream.
So here's my life-long wish, my
some-thing love - ly wrapped be-neath our tree.
Well, heav-en sure-ly knows that
Dm7
E♭(add2)
E♭
B♭/D
Cm7
Cm7/F
F
grown up Christ-mas list, not for my-self, _ but for a world _ in need.
pack-ag - es and bows can nev - er heal _ a hurt-ing hu - man soul.
G
Bm7/E
Em
C(add9)
C
Am9
Am9/D
No more lives _ torn a-part _ and wars would nev - er start _
Bm7
Em
Em/D
C(sus2)
D7sus
D7
D7sus
_ and time would heal _ all hearts.

G
Bm7/E
Em/D
C(add9)
C
Am7
Am7/D
And ev - 'ry - one would have _ a friend _ and right would al - ways
Bm7
Em7
Em7/D
C#m7(♭5)
F#7♭5(♭9)
F#7#5
Bm7
Em
Am7
D9
win and love would nev - er end. _ This is my grown _ up Christ - mas
1
G
C/G
D/G
G
B7/D#
Em
G/B
C
Am7
Dsus
D
D/C
list.
As
2
G
C/G
D/G
G
G7sus
Dm/C
C
Dm/C
C
list. _ What is _ this il - lu - sion called? The in-no-cence of youth. _ May-be

Em7
Em7/A
A
D
F♯sus
F♯
B
F♯
G♯m
on - ly in _ our blind be-lief _ can we ev - er find _ the truth.
D♯m7
E(add2)
B/D♯
C♯m7
F♯sus
F♯
A♭
Cm7/F
Fm/E♭
D♭maj7
B♭m7
B♭m7/E♭
No more lives _ torn a - part _ and wars would nev - er
Cm7
Fm7
Fm7/E♭
D♭
D♭/E♭
A♭
Cm7/F
Fm/E♭
start and time would heal _ all hearts.
And ev - 'ry-one would have _ a friend _

D♭(add9) D♭ B♭m7 B♭m7/E♭ Cm7 Fm7 Fm7/E♭
and right would al - ways win and love would nev - er
Dm7(♭5) G7♭9 D♭9(♯11) Cm7 Fm7 B♭m7 E♭7sus E♭7sus/D♭
end, oh. This is my grown up Christ - mas
Cm7 Fm7 Dm7♭5 D♭9(♯11) Cm7 Fm7 B♭m7 B♭m7/E♭ E♭7
list. This is my on - ly life - long wish. This is my grown up Christ - mas
A♭ E♭ Fm Cm7 D♭(add9) E♭ A♭/E♭ E♭7 A♭
list.

HAPPY CHRISTMAS, LITTLE FRIEND

Lyrics by OSCAR HAMMERSTEIN II
Music by RICHARD RODGERS

G7
C
A7
Moderately
mp
D7
G
D7
G
The soft morn-ing light of a pale win-ter sun is
G
D7
G
C
Am7
trac - ing the trees on the snow. Leap up lit - tle friend and
G/D
Em
Am7
D7
G
fly down the stairs for Christ - mas is wait - ing be - low. There's a

D
G
D
G
D
G7
tree in the room run - ning o - ver with stars that twin - kle and sing to your
C
Am7♭5
G/D
F7/C
G/B
Em7/B♭
eyes. And un - der the tree there are pre - sents that say un -
Am7
D7
G
Gmaj7
G
wrap me and get a sur - prise.
Slowly
Gmaj7
Am7
D7
G6
Hap - py Christ - mas, lit - tle friend, may your

Am7
D7
G6
G
Am7
heart be laugh - ing all day.
May your joy be a
D7
G
Am7
D7
dream you'll re - mem - ber,
as the years roll a - long on their
G6
G
Am7
D7
Gmaj7
way.
As the years roll a - long on their way
G6
Am7
D7
G/B
you'll be show - ing your own kid a tree.

Am7
D7
G6
Am7
Then at last, my friend, you'll know how hap - py a
D7
G7
Am7/C
Cmaj7/B
Christ - mas can be, how hap - py a
C(add9)/A
D7
1 G
Em
Am7
Christ - mas can be.
D7
2 G
C
G6
be.

HAPPY HOLIDAY

from the Motion Picture Irving Berlin's HOLIDAY INN

Words and Music by
IRVING BERLIN

Slowly
E♭maj7
Cm/B♭
Fm7
B♭7
E♭maj7
Cm/B♭
8va
mf
Fm7
B♭7
E♭
Hap - py hol - i - day,
hap - py
8va
Fm7
B♭7
hol - i - day.
While the mer - ry bells keep
8va
E♭
Cm7
Fm7
B♭7
E♭
ring - ing, may your ev - 'ry wish come true.
Hap - py

Fm7
hol - i - day,
hap - py hol - i - day.
8va
B♭7
E♭
Cm7
3 fr
May the cal - en - dar keep bring - ing hap - py
Fm7
B♭7
E♭
F7
B♭6
hol - i - days to you.
Hap - py hol - i - day,
Cm7
F7
hap - py hol - i - day.
While the

Cm
F7
B♭6
Gm7
Cm7
F7
mer - ry bells keep ring - ing, may your ev - 'ry wish come
B♭6
true. Hap - py hol - i - day, hap - py
8va
Cm7
F7
Cm7
F7
hol - i - day. May the cal - en - dar keep
8va
B♭6
Gm7
Cm7
F7
B♭6
bring - ing hap - py hol - i - days to you.

A HOLLY JOLLY CHRISTMAS

Music and Lyrics by
JOHNNY MARKS

Moderately bright
C
Dm7
mf
G7
C
C#dim
Have a hol - ly jol - ly Christ - mas, it's the best time of the year.
G7
C#dim
I don't know if there'll be snow, but
G7
C
G7
C
have a cup of cheer. Have a hol - ly jol - ly

C#dim
G7
Christ - mas, and when you walk down the street
C#dim
G7
say hel - lo to friends you know and ev - 'ry - one you
C
F
Em
F
meet. Oh, ho, the mis - tle - toe hung where you can
C
Dm
Am
D7
C/D
D7
see. Some - bod - y waits for you, kiss her once for

G7
C
me. Have a hol - ly jol - ly Christ - mas, and in
C♯dim
G7
case you did - n't hear, oh, by gol - ly, have a
C
1
D7
G7
C
G7
hol - ly jol - ly Christ - mas this year. Have a
2
D7
G7
C
Dm7
G7
C
Christ - mas this year.

HAPPY XMAS
(War Is Over)

Words and Music by JOHN LENNON
and YOKO ONO

A
Asus9
Asus4
A
So this is X - mas and what have you
X - mas and what have we
Bm
Bmsus9
Bmsus4
Bm
Bm7
E7
Bm7
E13
done? An - oth - er year ov - er, a new one just be -
done? An - oth - er year ov - er, a new one just be -
A
Asus9
Asus4
A13
D
Dmaj4
Dsus4
D
gun; And so this is X - mas, I hope you have
gun; And so hap - py X - mas, We hope you have
Em
Em(7♯)
Em9
Em
A
Asus9
A13
fun the near and the dear ones The old and the
fun the near and the dear ones The old and the

D
Dsus4
D13
young.
young.
A mer - ry, mer - ry
G
A
G
F#m
X - mas
And a hap - py New year,
let's hope it's a
Em
G
To Coda
D
E
E7
good one
with - out an - y fear.
And so this is
A
Amaj7
D6
A
Bm
Bm(7#)
Bm9
Bm
X - mas
for weak and for strong
The rich and the
(War is o - ver if you want it

E7sus4
E7
Bm7
E7
A
E7
Bb
A
poor ones the road is so long. And so, hap-py
war is o - ver now.
D
Dmaj7
G6
Em
Em(7#)
Em9
Em
X-mas for black and for white For the yel-low and
(War is o - ver if you want it
A7sus4
A7
Em7
A7
D
A7
Em
D13
red ones let's stop all the fights. A mer-ry, mer-ry
war is o - ver now
G
A
G
F#m
X-mas And a hap-py New Year. Let's hope it's a

Em
G
D
E
E13
D. S. al Coda
good one
with-out an - y
fear.
And so this is
CODA
D
E
E7
fear
A
Amaj7
D6
A
Bm
Bm(7♯)
Bm9
Bm
Was
is
o - ver
if
you
want
it
E7sus4
E7
Bm7
E7
A
E7
Bm
A
war
is
o - ver
now.

HARK! THE HERALD ANGELS SING

Words by CHARLES WESLEY
Altered by GEORGE WHITEFIELD
Music by FELIX MENDELSSOHN-BARTHOLDY
Arranged by WILLIAM H. CUMMINGS

Joyfully
f
G
G/D
D
Hark! The Her - ald An - gels Sing,
G/B
Bm
C
G/D
D7
G
"Glo - ry to the new - born King! Peace on earth, and
Em
A7/C#
D
A7/E
D
D/A
A7
D
mer - cy mild, God and sin - ners re - con - ciled."

G
D7/F#
G
G/D
D
G
Joy - ful all ye na - tions rise,
Join the tri - umph
D7/F#
G
D
C
E7/B
Am
E7
Am
of the skies;
With th' an - gel - ic host pro - claim,
D7
G/B
G/D
D7
G
C
E7/B
"Christ is born in Beth - le - hem."
Hark! The Her - ald
Am
E7
Am
D7
G/B
G/D
D7
G
An - gels Sing, "Glo - ry to the new - born King!"

HOLLY LEAVES AND CHRISTMAS TREES

Words and Music by RED WEST and GLEN SPREEN

Moderately slow

mp

C Dm G7

Some-where in, in the dis-tant night I hear

mp

C Am Dm

Christ-mas bells. The gen-tle snow keeps fall-ing down on

F C

peo-ple who are home-ward bound. That's the way it's

Dm
G7
C
al-ways been; the cir-cle nev-er real-ly ends.
Am
Dm
F
Christ-mas seems to come and go, home's a place that
C
G
C
I don't know. Hol-ly Leaves And Christ-mas Trees,
G
C
Am
it's that time of year, lights a-glow and

Em
F
G
mis-tle-toe don't mean a thing when you're not here.
C
Dm
G7
As I walk, walk this lone-ly street, the sound of snow be-
C
Am
Dm
neath my feet. I, think of how, how it used to be, when
F
G7
F
Hol-ly Leaves And Christ-mas Trees used to mean so
C
F
(C Bass)
C
much to me.
rit.

HOW LOVELY IS CHRISTMAS

Words by ARNOLD SUNDGAARD
Music by ALEC WILDER

Gently
C Dm7 G7
mp
With pedal
C G7 C F C
How love - ly is Christ - mas with boughs in the
love - ly is Christ - mas when chil - dren are
F6 C Dm7 G7
hall, when bells rin - gle jin - gle and friends come to
near, the sound of their laugh - ter, sweet sea - son of
C G7 C F C
call. How love - ly is Christ - mas with joy on the
cheer. How love - ly is Christ - mas with gifts by the

F6
C
Dm7
G7
wing, while un - der your win - dow the car - ol - ers
tree, each gift tells a sto - ry; oh, what will it
Em7♭5
A
D/F♯
A7/E
D
A/C♯
sing, "God rest ye, be mer - ry, give peace where you
be? The yule log is burn - ing, the stars gleam a -
D
Gm/B♭
D7sus/A
Gm
C/E
G7/D
C
Bm7♭5
may; re - mem - ber the Child who was born on this
bove, re - mem - ber the gift of the Christ Child is
E7
G7
C
F
day." How love - ly is Christ - mas, with
love. The bells ring for Christ - mas, our

C F6 C Dm7
songs in the air, a brigbt Mer - ry Christ - mas, dear
sto - ry now ends, good night, Mer - ry Christ - mas, dear
G7 C G7 C G7 C
1 2
friends ev - 'ry - where. How
neigh - bors and friends. How love - ly is
F C F6
Christ - mas with songs in the air, a
C Dm7 G7 C
bright Mer - ry Christ - mas, dear friends ev - 'ry - where.
rit.

I SAW THREE SHIPS

Traditional English Carol
Spirited
I saw three ships come sail - ing in, On Christ - mas Day, on Christ - mas Day; I
what was in those ships all three, On Christ - mas Day, on Christ - mas Day; And
saw three ships come sail - ing in, On Christ - mas Day in the morn - ing. And
what was in those ships all three, On Christ - mas Day in the morn - ing. The
Vir - gin Mar - y and Christ were there, On
Christ - mas Day, on Christ - mas Day; The Vir - gin Mar - y and Christ were there, On Christ - mas Day in the morn - ing.

I'LL BE HOME FOR CHRISTMAS

Words and Music by KIM GANNON
and WALTER KENT

Moderately slow
Cmaj7
Em7
Dm7
mf
G7
F
Em7
Dm7
Am7
I'm dream - ing to - night of a place I love, e - ven
3
Dm7
D♭
Cmaj7
F
Em7
more than I u - sual - ly do. And al - though I know it's a
Dm7
Am7
D7
Dm7/G
G7♯5
long road back, I prom - ise you

C
E♭dim7
Dm7
Gsus
3fr
G7
I'll be home for Christ - mas,
Em7♭5
A7
Dm7
G7
you can count on me.
Fm
G7♭9
4fr
Cmaj7
Am7
Please have snow and mis - tle - toe and
D7
A♭dim7
4fr
Dm7/G
G7
pres - ents on the tree.

C
E♭dim7
Dm7
Gsus
G7
Em7♭5
Christ - mas Eve will find me where the
A7
Dm7
F6
Fm6
love - light gleams. I'll be home for
Em
A7
D7
Dm7
G7♭9
Christ - mas, if on - ly in my
1
C
Dm7
G7♯5
dreams.
2
C
dreams.
rit.

I WONDER AS I WANDER

By JOHN JACOB NILES

Espressivo
N.C.
I
p
Gm
Cm/G
Gm7
Cm/G
won - der as I wan - der out un - der the sky, how
mp
Gm
Cm/G
Gm7
Cm/G
Gm
Je - sus the Sav - ior did come for to die for
Cm/G
Gm7
G7
poor on - 'ry peo - ple like you and like I... I
f

Cm B♭/D Cm7 Gm Gm6 Cm
won - der as I wan - der out un - der the sky. When
rit. p più lento
Gm Cm/G Gm7 D7/F♯ Gm Cm/G
Mar - y birthed Je - sus, 'twas in a cow's stall, with wise men and far - mers and
mp a tempo
Gm7 Cm/G Gm Cm/G
shep - herds and all. But high from God's heav - en a
f
Gm7 G7/D Cm Gm/B♭ Cm7 B♭/D Cm6/9 E♭/B♭
star's light did fall, and the prom - ise of ag - es it
mp rit. f più lento

Gm7 Gm6 Cm Gm Cm/G Gm7 D7♭5/F# D/F#
then did re - call. If Je - sus had want - ed for an - y wee thing, a
p
a tempo
Gm Cm/G Gm7 Cm/G Gm
star in the sky or a bird on the wing, or
Cm/G Gm G7
all of God's an - gels in heav'n for to sing, He
f
Cm Gm/B♭ Cm7 B♭/D Cm6/9 E♭/B♭ Gm Gm6 Cm
sure - ly could have it, 'cause He was the King. I
rit.
p
più lento
f
mp

Gm
Cm/G
Gm7
Cm/G
won - der as I wan - der out un - der the sky, how
Gm
Cm/G
Gm7
Cm/G
Gm
Je - sus the Sav - ior did come for to die for
pp
Cm/G
Gm7
G7
poor on - 'ry peo - ple like you and like I... I
Cm
B♭/D
Cm7
Gm
Gm6
Cm
Gm
won - der as I wan - der out un - der the sky.
rit.
più lento

I'LL BE HOME ON CHRISTMAS DAY

Words and Music by
MICHAEL JARRETT

Moderately slow
E
Esus
E
mf
Esus
E
From the hills of Geor - gia,
It's been so man - y times be - fore
There were times I'd think a - bout her,
E7
a - cross the plains of Ten - nes - see,
she left that can - dle burn -
all the love I left be -
A

B
ing. I've seen and I've done
hind. And all too
And mem - o - ries
most ev - 'ry - thing that a
man - y tears that fell, my
still lin - ger with -
E
man can do or see.
soul filled with yearn - ing.
in my trou - bled mind.
But if I could on - ly
If I had an - y sense
If I could set a - side

E7
A
bor - row one dream
at all, I'd just be
my pride, then I'd be
from yes - ter - day, I'd
on my way. I'd
on my way. I'd
B
be on that train to - mor - row.
be on that train to - mor - row.
catch that train to mor - row.
I'll be home on Christ - mas

E
1,2
3
day.
If
E
E7
I had
an - y sense at all,
A
I'd just be
on my
B
way.
I'd catch that train

to - mor - row.
I'll be
1
home on
E
Christ - mas day.
2
I said, I'll home on
N.C.
E
Christ - mas day.

IT CAME UPON THE MIDNIGHT CLEAR

Words by EDMUND HAMILTON SEARS
Music by RICHARD STORRS WILLIS

Quietly
mp
Bb
Bb+
Eb/Bb
It
Came
Up - on
The
Bb
Eb
Mid - night
Clear,
That
glo - rious
C7
F
F7
Bb
song
of
old,
From

Bb+
Eb/Bb
Bb
an - gels bend - ing near the
Eb
Cm7
F7
earth, To touch their harps of
Bb
Taceт
D
gold; "Peace on the
D7
Gm
D
Gm
earth, good will to men, From

F/C
C7
F
heaven's all - gra - cious King."
F7
B♭
B♭+
E♭/B♭
The world in sol - emn
B♭
E♭
Cm7
still - ness lay, To hear the
F7
B♭
an - gels sing.

I'M SPENDING CHRISTMAS WITH YOU

Words and Music by
TOM OCCHIPINTI

Country Swing Waltz
A♭
B♭7
Gm
C
mf
Fm7
B♭
E♭
B♭7
E♭
Cm
The snow is gen - tly fall - ing, the
fire - place is burn - ing, and your
A♭
A♭m
E♭
night is so cold. The moon shines on the
hands feel so warm. The pres - ents are

F7
Fm7
B♭7
Cm
B♭7/D
3fr
snow covered trees. And the
un - der our tree. And I
E♭
Cm
A♭
4fr
road seemed like for - ev - er, but I'm fi - n'ly
take you in my arms, and your lips are touch - ing
A♭m
E♭
A♭/B♭
home. We're a - lone on this Christ - mas
mine. And it feels like our first Christ - mas
E♭
E♭7
A♭
Eve.
Eve.
I'm spend - ing

B♭7
E♭
3fr
Christ - mas with you.
It's the
Cm
3fr
F7
Fm7
sea - son when love is re - newed.
Cm
Gm
E♭/B♭
A♭
B♭7
3fr
3fr
4fr
My hol - i - day wish - es have al -
Gm
C7
Fm7
3fr
read - y come true.
I'm spend - ing

B♭7
1
E♭
B♭7
Cm
B♭7/D
2
E♭
Christ - mas __ with you. The you.
Cm
Gm
E♭/B♭
A♭
B♭7
Gm
My hol - i - day wish - es __ have al - read - y come __
C7
Fm7
B♭7
E♭
true. __ I'm spend - ing Christ - mas __ with you.
Cm
A♭
A♭m6
E♭

I'VE GOT MY LOVE TO KEEP ME WARM

from the 20th Century Fox Motion Picture ON THE AVENUE

Words and Music by
IRVING BERLIN

Bright jump tempo
E♭6/B♭
F♯dim/B♭
B♭7
E♭6/B♭
F♯dim/B♭
mp
B♭7sus
B♭7
E♭/G
G♭dim
G♭m6
G♭dim
Fm
The snow is snow - ing, the wind is
B♭7♭5
A♭/B♭
B♭9
Am7♭5
D7
D7♭9
blow - ing, but I can weath - er the storm.
F♯dim
Fm7
B♭7
B♭9sus
What do I care how much it may storm?

B♭9
E♭/G
B7/F♯
Fm7
B♭9
E♭6
G♭dim
I've got my love to keep me warm.
Fm7
B♭7
E♭/G
G♭dim
G♭m6
G♭dim
Fm
I can't re - mem - ber a worse De -
B♭7♭5
A♭/B♭
B♭9
Am7♭5
D7
D7♭9
cem - ber; just watch those i - ci - cles form.
F♯dim
Fm7
B♭7
B♭9sus
What do I care if i - ci - cles form?

B♭9
E♭/G
B7/F♯
Fm7
B♭9
E♭6
I've got my love to keep me warm.
D7♭9
Gm
D+
Off with my o - ver - coat,
Gm7
C7
Fm
G7
C7
off with my glove.
I need no o - ver - coat,
Fm
Fm7♭5
B♭7
Fm7/C
B♭7/D
E♭/G
G♭dim
G♭m6
G♭dim
I'm burn-ing with love.
My heart's on fire, the

Fm
B♭7♭5
A♭/B♭
B♭9
Am7♭5
D7
D7♭9
flame grows high - er. So I will weath - er the storm.
F♯dim
Fm7
B♭7
What do I care how much it may storm?
B♭9sus
B♭9
E♭/G
B7/F♯
Fm7
B♭9
I've got my love to keep me warm.
1 E♭
G♭dim7
Fm9
B♭7/D
The
2 E♭
D♭6/9
E♭6

IT MUST HAVE BEEN THE MISTLETOE
(Our First Christmas)

By JUSTIN WILDE
and DOUG KONECKY

Moderately
F(add9)
B♭maj7
8va
F(add9)
mp
C7sus
F(add9)
8va
loco
It must have been the mis - tle - toe, the
F(add9)/A
B♭(add9)
la - zy fire, the fall - ing snow, the ma - gic in the frost - y air, that
B♭/C
F(add9)
feel - ing ev - 'ry - where. It must have been the pret - ty lights that

Cm7
E♭/F
B♭maj7
Gm7
glis - tened in the si - lent night, or may - be just the stars so bright that
B♭/C
B♭maj7
Fmaj7
shined a - bove you. Our first Christ - mas,
mf
Gm7
C9
Fmaj7
more than we'd been dream - ing of.
B♭m7
E♭9
Cm7
Fm7
Old Saint Nich - 'las
f

B♭7sus
B♭7
B♭/C
C
B♭/C
had his fin - gers crossed, that we would fall in love. _ It
F(add9)
F(add9)/A
could have been _ the hol - i - day, _ the mid - night ride _ up - on a sleigh, _ the
mp
B♭(add9)
B♭/C
coun - try - side _ all dressed in white, _ that cra - zy snow - ball fight. It
F(add9)
Cm7
E♭/F
could have been _ the stee - ple bell _ that wrapped us up with - in its spell. _ It

B♭maj7
Gm7
B♭/C
C6
on - ly took one kiss to know, it must have been the
F(add9)
B♭maj7
Fmaj7
mis - tle - toe. Our first Christ - mas,
mf
Gm7
C9
Fmaj7
more than we'd been dream - ing of.
B♭m7
E♭9
Cm7
Fm7
Old Saint Nich - 'las
f

B♭7sus
B♭7
D♭/E♭
must have known that kiss would lead to all of this. It
A♭(add9)
A♭(add9)/C
must have been the mis - tle - toe, the la - zy fire, the fall - ing snow, the
D♭(add9)
D♭/E♭
mag - ic in the frost - y air, that made me love you. On
A♭(add9)
E♭m7
G♭/A♭
Christ - mas Eve a wish came true, that night I fell in love with you. It

D♭(add9)
B♭m7
D♭/E♭
on - ly took one kiss to know, it must have been the
A♭(add9)
A♭(add9)/C
B♭m7
E♭6
mis - tle - toe! It must have been the
mf
rit.
Freely
Fm
Fm(maj7)
Fm7
Fm6
B♭m7
D♭/E♭
mis - tle - toe! It must have been the
mp
A♭(add9)
D♭maj7
A♭(add9)
mis - tle - toe!
8va
a tempo
rit.

IT WON'T SEEM LIKE CHRISTMAS
(Without You)

Words and Music by
J.A. BALTHROP

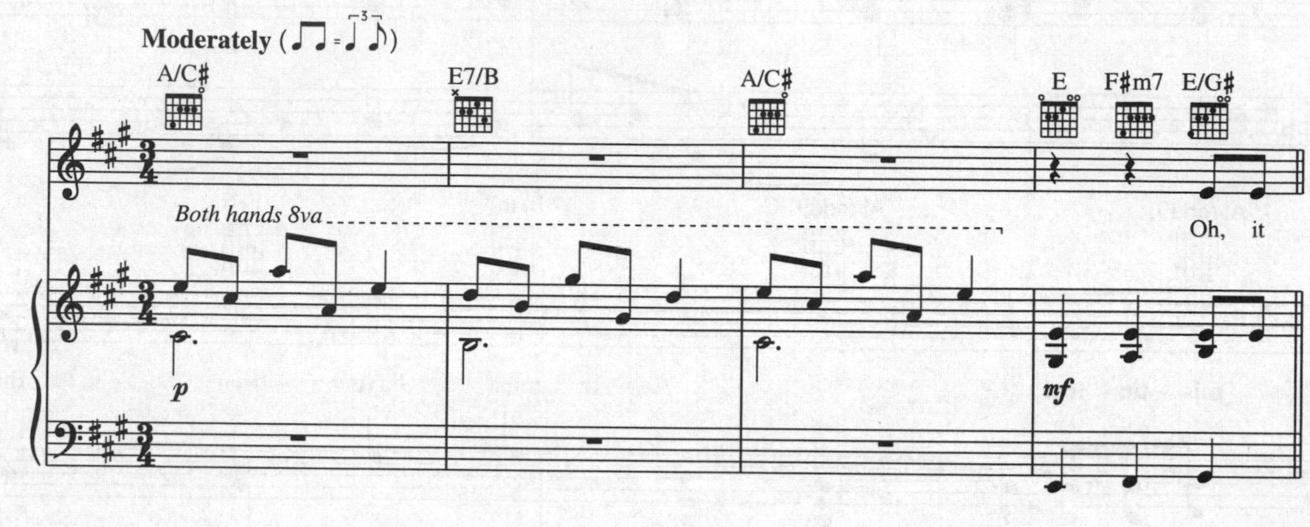
Moderately
A/C#
E7/B
A/C#
E
F#m7
E/G#
Both hands 8va
Oh, it
p
mf

A
D
A
won't seem like Christ-mas, oh, with-out you, for

A7
D
too man-y miles are be-tween. But if I

D♯dim7
A/E
A
get the one thing that I'm wish-ing for
then I'll
E7
To Coda
A
F♯dim7
E7/G♯
see you to-night in my dreams.
Seems a
A
D
A
long time since we've been to-geth-er;
it was
A7
D
just a-bout to this time of year.
Looks like

D♯dim7
A/E
A
it's gon - na be snow - y wea - ther.
How I
E7
A
D.S. al Coda
E
F♯m
E7/G♯
wish that you could be here.
But it
CODA
A
F
Gm
3fr
F/A
B♭
E♭
3fr
dreams.
In the dis - tance
I hear sleigh bells
B♭
B♭7
ring - ing.
The hol - ly's so pret - ty this

E♭
3fr
Edim7
year
and the car - ol
that some - bod - y's
B♭/F
B♭
F7
sing - ing
a - re - minds me
of our Christ - mas last
B♭
B♭/F
G7sus
F7/A
3fr
B♭
E♭
3fr
year.
Oh, but it won't
be like Christ - mas
with -
B♭
B♭7
out you
for too
man - y miles
are be -

Eb
3fr
Edim7
3
tween.
Oh, but if I
get the
one thing
that I'm
Bb/F
Bb
F7
wish-ing for
then I'll
see you
to - night
in my
Bb
F/A
Gm7
F7
dreams.
Yes, I'll
see
you
to -
Slower
Bb
Eb
Bb/F
Cm/G
Bb/F
Eb
Bb
night
in
my
dreams.

IT'S BEGINNING TO LOOK LIKE CHRISTMAS

By MEREDITH WILLSON
In a Moderate Tempo
mf
Ab
Db
Ab
It's be - gin - ning to look a lot like Christ - mas,
p
C7
Db
F7
ev - 'ry - where you go;
Take a
There's a
Bbm
Eb7
Ab
B7
look in the five and ten, glis - ten- ing once a -gain, with
tree in the grand ho - tel, one in the park, as well, the

E♭ Edim B♭7 B♭m7 E♭7

can - dy canes and sil - ver lanes a - glow.
stur - dy kind that does - n't mind the snow. It's be -

A♭ D♭ A♭

gin -ning to look a lot like Christ - mas,

C7 D♭ F7

toys in ev - 'ry store. But the
soon the bells will start. And the

B♭m7 Bdim A♭ A♭7 F7

pret - ti - est sight to see is the hol - ly that will be, on your
thing that will make them ring is the ca - rol that you sing right with -

Bbm7
Eb7
1. Ab
To Patter
2. Ab
Fine
own front door A pair of
in your heart
Patter
C7
Fm
C7
Fm
hop-a-long boots and a pis-tol that shoots is the wish of Bar-ney and Ben;
Bb7
Eb
Bb7
Eb
Dolls that will talk and will go for a walk is the hope of Jan-ice and Jen; And
Eb7
Edim
Eb7
D.S. al Fine
Mom and Dad can hard-ly wait for school to start a-gain. It's be-
mf
p

IT'S CHRISTMAS TIME ALL OVER THE WORLD

Words and Music by
HUGH MARTIN

Fast and gaily
mf
mp
Eb6 D7-9 Db9-5 C9 F9 add D F+9 Bb9 add G
It's Christ-mas Time All O-ver The World, — And Christ-mas here at home. —
Eb6 D7-9 Db9-5 C9 F+7 Bb9 Eb+9 Fm7 Ab6 G7-9 Gb9-5 F9
The church bells chime wher-ev-er we roam, — So Joy-eux No-ël, Fe-liz Na-
(Zhwah-yuh No-el) (Feh-leez Nah-
Gm7-5 C7 Fm7 Bb7 Eb maj.7 Eb6 Dm7-5 G7

Cm7 F7 Ab Ab6 Fm7 Fb9 Eb Ebmaj.9
tal, Gel - luk - kig Kerst - feest to you!
tahl) (Huh - lukh - kuh Kairst - feest)
Eb Eb6 Fm7 Bb9 Bb7 Eb6 D7-9 Db9-5 C9 F9 add D F+9 Bb9 add G
The snow is thick in most of the world
Eb6 D7-9 Db9-5 C9 F+7 Bb9 Eb+9 Fm7 Ab6 G7-9 Gb9-5 F9
And chil - dren's eyes are wide As old Saint Nick gets
Gm7-5 C7 Fm7 Bb7 Ebmaj.7 Eb6 Dm7-5 G7
read - y to ride, So Fe - liz Nav - i - dad, Crăciun Fe - ri -
(Feh - lees Nah - vee dahd) Krah - choon Feh - ree -
Cm7 F7 Ab Ab6 Fm7 Fb9 Eb Ebmaj.9
cit, and Hap - py New Year to you!
cheet)

E♭ E♭6 E♭maj.9 E♭6 Dm7-5 G7
Though the cus - toms may
mp
Cm add D Cm6 Fm7 B♭7 E♭maj.9
change, And the lan - guage is strange,
E♭6 Am7-5 D7 Gm add A Gm
This ap - peal we feel is real in Hol - land or
Fm7 B♭7 E♭6 D7-9
Hong Kong. It's Christ - mas
mf
mp
D♭9-5 C9 F9addD F+9 B♭9addG E♭6 D7-9 D♭9-5 C9 F+7 B♭9 E♭+9
Time All O - ver The World, In plac - es near and far;

Fm7 A♭6 G7-9 G♭9-5 F9 Gm7-5 C7 Fm7 B♭7
And so, my friends, wher - ev - er you are, A Fröh - li - che Weih -
(Fruh - lee-kheh Vy -
E♭maj.7 E♭6 Dm7-5 G7 Cm7 F7 B♭m7 E♭7
nacht - en! Ka - la Christ - ou - ge - na! Yo - i Kurisu -
nakh - ten) (Kah - lah Hrees - too - yeh - nah) (Yo - ee Kreess -
A♭maj.7 A♭6 A♭ Fm7 1. Fm9 B♭7-9 E♭6 E♭maj.9
ma - su! Which means a ver - y mer - ry Christ - mas to you!
mah - soo)
mf
E♭ E♭6 Fm7 B♭9 B♭7 2. Fm9
It's Christ - mas
mp
8va
B♭+7-9 E♭ E♭maj.7 E♭ E♭6 Fm7 E♭
to you!
loco
mf
f
ff
sfz
8va

IT'S JUST ANOTHER NEW YEAR'S EVE

Lyric by MARTY PANZER
Music by BARRY MANILOW

Slow ballad
F(add9)
Gm11/F
mf
F(add9)
Gm11/F
Don't look _ so sad. _
rit.
Em7
A7♭5
A7
Dm7
D♭m7 Cm7
F9
It's not ___ so bad, _ you know. _ It's just an-oth-er
but we've _ made good _ friends, too. ___ Re-mem-ber all the
lone, we've got ___ the world, _ you know. _ And it won't let us
a tempo

B♭maj7
A7♭5
A7
Dm7
D♭m7
Cm7
F9
night, that's all it is. It's not the first.
nights we've spent with them and all our plans.
down, just wait and see. And we'll grow old,
B♭maj7
C7/B♭
Am7
Dm7
It's not the worst you know. We've come through all
Who says they can't come true? To-night's an-oth-
but think how wise we'll grow There's more you know,
1
G9sus
G7
C9
the rest. We'll get through this. We've made mis-takes

2,3
G7sus
G7
C9sus
B7
- er chance _ to start a - gain.
_ it's on - ly New _ Year's Eve. _
It's just an - oth -
B♭maj7
C7
C7/B♭
Am7♭5
D7♭9
D7
- er New Year's Eve, _ an - oth - er night _ like all _ the rest.
It's just an - oth -
Gm7
C7
Fmaj7
B9
- er New _ Year's Eve, _ let's make it the best.
It's just an - oth -
B♭maj7
C7
C7/B♭
Am7♭5
D7
- er New Year's Eve _ it's just an - oth - er Auld _ Lang Syne. _
But when we're through, _

To Coda

Gm7 Am7 F/A B♭maj7 B♭maj7/C

this New Year you'll see we'll be just

F(add9) Fsus F Dm7 Gm7 C9

fine.

Am7 Dm7 Gm9 B♭maj7 B♭maj7/C

D.S. al Coda

CODA

We're not a- we'll be just

rit.

F(add9) B♭/F Fmaj7

fine.

8va

a tempo

rit.

JESUS BORN ON THIS DAY

Words and Music by MARIAH CAREY
and WALTER AFANASIEFF

Moderately slow
Gmaj7/B
A/C#
Dsus
mp
D
D
Gmaj7/B
A/C#
D
To - day a child is _ born on earth. (To - day a
Be - hold the Lamb of _ God has come. (Be - hold the
To - day our hearts re - joice in Him. (To - day our
Gmaj7/B
A/C#
D
G/B
Gm/Bb
child is _ born on earth.) To - day the glo - ry of God _
Lamb of _ God has come.) Be - hold the Sav - ior is born. _
hearts re - joice in Him.) To - day the light of His birth _
Bm
E/G#
A
A/C#
D
shines ev - 'ry - where _ for _ all of the world. _
Sing of His love _ to _ ev - 'ry - one. _
fills us with hope _ and _ brings peace on earth. _
Oh, Je - sus, _

A♯dim Bm E/G♯ A E/G♯ A
born on this day, __ (1.,3.) He is our light __ and sal - va - tion. __ Oh,
(2.) Heav-en-ly child __ in a man - ger. __ Oh,
A/C♯ D A♯dim Bm E/G♯ A E
Je - sus, __ born on this day, __ He is the King __ of all na -
Je - sus, __ born on this day, __ He is our Lord __ and our Sav -
1,2 A 3 A F
- tions. __ - tions. __ To - day a
- ior. ___
B♭maj7/D C/E F B♭maj7/D C/E
child is __ born on earth. (To - day a child is __ born on

F
B♭/D
C/E
earth.) He is light, He is love, He is grace, born on Christ - mas
F
B♭/D
B♭
C
day. He is light, He is love, He is grace, born on Christ - mas
F
1
B♭/D
B♭
C
day. He is light, He is love, He is grace, born on Christ - mas
2
B♭/D
B♭
C
F
B♭maj7/D
5fr
C/E
F
He is grace, born on Christ - mas day.
rit.

JESUS WHAT A WONDERFUL CHILD

Arrangement by MARIAH CAREY,
WALTER AFANASIEFF and LORIS HOLLAND

Freely
Gospel swing
F C7 F C7 D7♭9 G7♭9 C7 F
4fr
mf
B♭/C F
Jesus, Jesus,
B♭7 F Em7 A7
oh, what a wonderful child. Jesus,
Dm G C7
Jesus, so lowly meek and mild. New

F
B♭7
Bdim7
life, new hope, new joy He brings. Won't you lis-ten to the an-gels sing
F/C
C7/B♭
F/A
C7/G
F♯dim
G7
C7
F
To Coda
glo-ry, glo-ry, glo - ry to the new born King.
1
B♭/C
2
B♭/C
F
He was her-ald by the
B♭
E♭7
F
an-gels, born in a low-ly man-ger. The

Em7
A7
Dm
Gsus
G7
Vir-gin Mar-y was His moth - er and Jo-seph was His earth - ly fa -
C7
F
- ther. Three wise men came from a - far. They were
B♭
G7
B♭m6
6fr
F/C
C7/B♭
guid-ed by a shin - ing star to see King Je - sus where He
Am7♭5
D7
G7
C7
Gm7
3 fr
F
B♭/C
D.S. al Coda
lay in a man-ger filled with hay. Oh,

CODA
F
B♭7
Je - sus,
Lead vocal ad lib.
Je - sus,
1
2
C♭/D♭
Je - sus,
G♭
C♭7
C/D
G
C7

G
C7
1
Je - sus,
Je - sus,
Je - sus,
2
G/B
D/F#
F7
E7
Glo - ry,
glo - ry,
glo - ry to the
A7
D7
Much Faster!
new born King.
Repeat ad lib. and Fade
Je - sus.

JINGLE-BELL ROCK

Words and Music by JOE BEAL
and JIM BOOTHE

Brightly
C
G
mp
Moderately, with a swing
C
C#dim7
Jin - gle - bell, jin - gle - bell, jin - gle - bell rock, __ jin - gle - bell swing and
mf
Dm7
G7
Dm7
G7
Dm7
G7
jin - gle - bells ring. Snow - in' and blow - in' up bush - els of fun;
Dm7
G7
G7#5
C
now the jin - gle - hop has be - gun. __ Jin - gle - bell, jin - gle - bell,

C#dim7
Dm7
G7
jin - gle - bell rock, jin - gle - bells chime in jin - gle - bell time,
Dm7
G7
Dm7
G7
D7
G7
danc - in' and pranc - in' in Jin - gle - bell Square in the frost - y air.
C
C7
F
F#dim7
What a bright time, it's the right time to
C/G
C
Am7
D9
4fr
Am7
D9
4fr
rock the night a - way. Jin - gle - bell time is a swell time

G7
Dm7
G7
C
to go glid - in' in a one - horse sleigh. __
Gid - dy - ap, jin - gle horse,
Em7♭5/B♭
A7♯5
F
pick up your feet, __
jin - gle a - round the clock.
Mix and min - gle in a
Fm
D7
G7
1
C
C♯dim
Dm7
G7
jin - gl - in' beat, __
that's the jin - gle - bell rock.
that's the jin - gle - bell,
2
D7
G
D7
G7
C
Dm7
B
C
that's the jin - gle - bell, that's the jin - gle - bell rock. __

JINGLE BELLS

Words and Music by
J. PIERPONT

Bright 2
G
mf
Dash - ing through the snow in a one - horse o - pen
day or two a - go I thought I'd take a
Now the ground is white; go it while you're
C
Am
D7
sleigh, o'er the fields we go,
ride, and soon Miss Fan - nie Bright was
young. Take the girls to - night and
G
laugh - ing all the way. Bells on bob - tail
seat - ed by my side. The horse was lean and
sing this sleigh - ing song. Just get a bob - tail

ring, mak - ing spir - its
lank, mis - for - tune seemed his
bay, two - for - ty for his
C
Am
G/D
bright; what fun it is to ride and sing a
lot; he got in - to a drift - ed bank and
speed, then hitch him to an o - pen sleigh and
D7
G
D7
G
sleigh - ing song to - night! Oh!
we, we got up - sot! Oh!
crack! you'll take the lead! Oh!
Jin - gle bells,
G7
jin - gle bells, jin - gle all the way.

C
G
A7
Oh, what fun it is to ride in a one - horse o - pen
D7
G
sleigh! Hey! Jin - gle bells, jin - gle bells,
G7
C
jin - gle all the way. Oh, what fun it
G
D7
G
is to ride in a one - horse o - pen sleigh!
A

JOLLY OLD ST. NICHOLAS

Traditional 19th Century American Carol

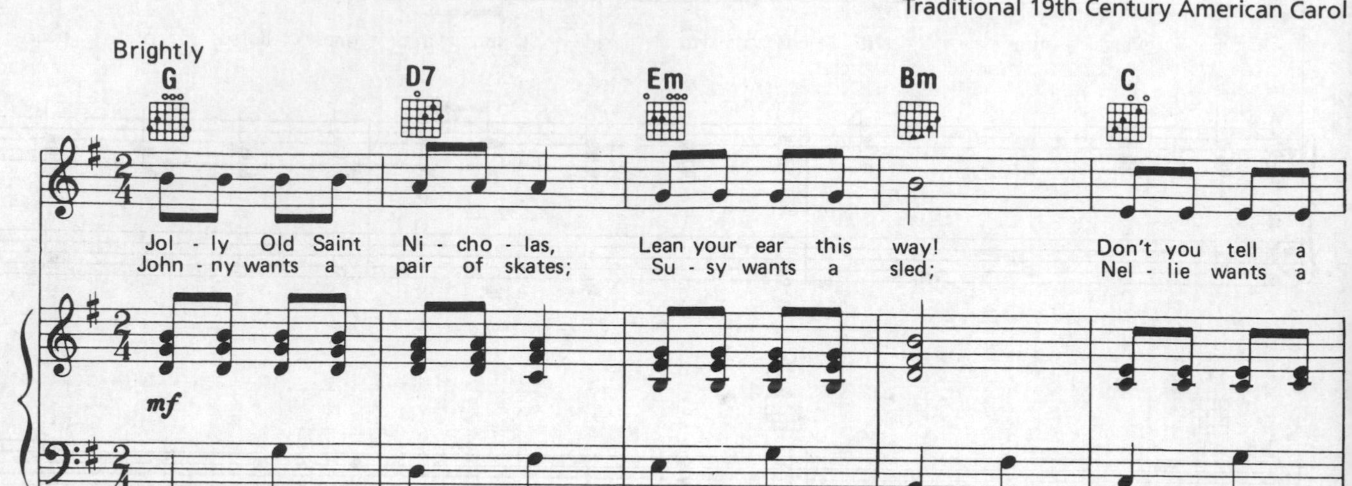
Brightly
G
D7
Em
Bm
C
mf
Jol - ly Old Saint Ni - cho - las, Lean your ear this way! Don't you tell a
John - ny wants a pair of skates; Su - sy wants a sled; Nel - lie wants a

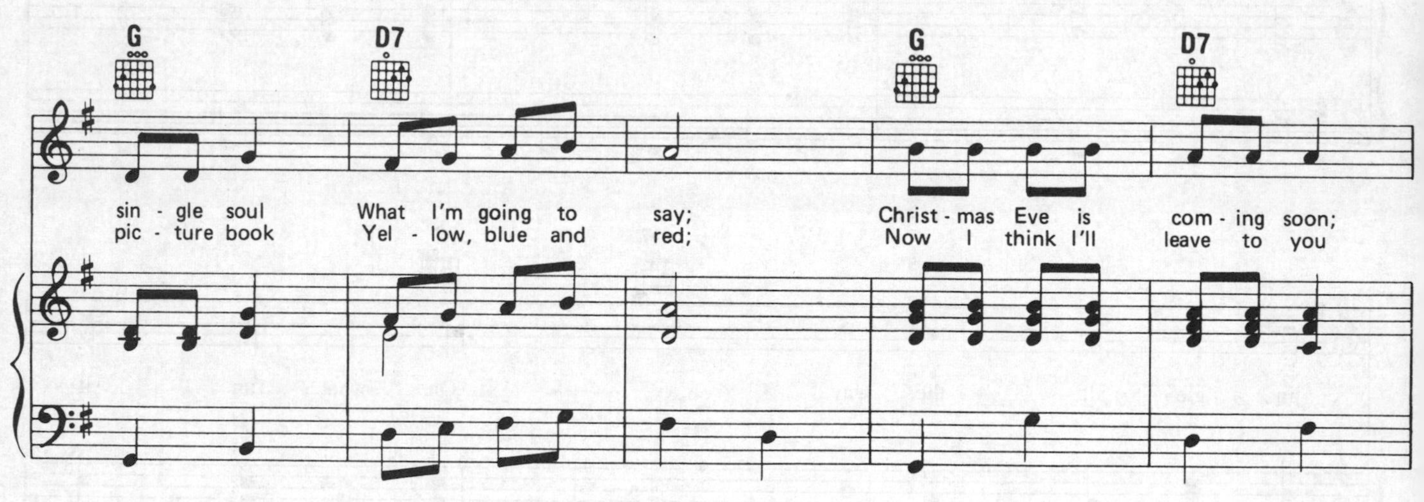
G
D7
G
D7
sin - gle soul What I'm going to say; Christ - mas Eve is com - ing soon;
pic - ture book Yel - low, blue and red; Now I think I'll leave to you

Em
Bm
C
G
D7
G
Now you dear old man, Whis - per what you'll bring to me; Tell me, if you can.
What to give the rest; Choose for me, dear San - ta Claus, You will know the best.

JOY TO THE WORLD

Words by ISAAC WATTS
Music by GEORGE FRIDERIC HANDEL
Arranged by LOWELL MASON

With spirit
D
G6
D/A
A
D
f
D
Em
D/A
A
D
Joy to the world! The Lord is come: Let
G
A7
D
earth re - ceive her King; Let ev - ery

heart prepare Him room, And heav-en and na-ture
sing, And heav-en and na-ture sing, And
heav-en and heav-en and na-ture sing.
He rules the world with truth and grace, And
A
D
G
D
Em
D/A
A
D
Em
D/A
A
D

G
A7
D
makes the na - tions prove The glo - ries
of His right - eous - ness, And won - ders of His
A
love, And won - ders of His love, And
D
G
D
Em
D/A
A
D
won - ders, won - ders of His love.

LAST CHRISTMAS

Words and Music by
GEORGE MICHAEL

Slowly and freely
Em7
Am7
Em7
mf
3
3
Am7
Fm6
Gsus
G
Spoken: Happy Christmas
3
Moderately steady beat
Cmaj9
C6
Cmaj9
C6
Em7/A
Am7
Em7/A
Am7
Ah,
oo,
woh,

Am7/D
Dm7
Am7/D
Dm7
ah.
Fmaj7/G
G9
Fmaj7/G
G9
Cmaj9
C6
Cmaj9
C6
Last Christ - mas I gave you my heart, but the
Em7/A
Am7
Em7/A
Am7
ver - y next day you gave it a - way.

Am7/D
Dm7
Am7/D
Dm7
This year to save me from tears I'll
Fmaj7/G
G9
1,3,5
To Coda
Fmaj7/G
G9
2,4
Fmaj7/G
G9
give it to some - one spe - cial. - cial.
Cmaj9
C6
Cmaj9
C6
Em7/A
Am7
Em7/A
Am7
Am/D
Dm7
Am/D
Dm

Fmaj7/G
G9
Fmaj7/G
G7
Cmaj9
C6
Cmaj9
C6
Once bit - ten and twice shy,
A crowd - ed room, friends with tired eyes.
Em7/A
Am7
Em7/A
Am7
I keep my dis - tance but tears still catch my eye.
I'm hid - ing from you And your soul of ice.
Am7/D
Dm7
Am7/D
Dm7
Tell me, ba - by, do you re - cog - nize me?
My god, I thought you were some - one to re - ly on.

Fmaj7/G
G9
Fmaj7/G
G9
Well, it's been a year. It does-n't sur-prise me.
Me, I guess I was a shoul-der to cry on. A
Cmaj9
C6
Cmaj9
C6
Hap-py Christ-mas. I wrapped it up and sent it
face on a lov-er with a fire in his heart, a
Em7/A
Am7
Em/A
Am7
with a note say-ing, "I love you." I meant it.
man un-der cov-er but you tore me a-
Am7/D
Dm7
Am7/D
Dm7
Now I know what a fool I've been. But if you
part. Oo, now I've

Fmaj7/G
G7
1
2
D.S. al Coda
(with repeat)
kissed me now I know you'd fool me a - gain.
found a real love. You'll nev - er
fool me a - gain.
CODA
Cmaj9
C6
- cial.
A face on a lov - er with a
Em7/A
Am7
fire in his heart, a man un - der cov - er but you
Am7/D
Dm7
tore him a - part. May - be next year I'll

Fmaj7/G
G9
Fmaj7/G
G9
give it to some - one, I'll give it to some - one spe -
Cmaj9
C6
Cmaj9
C6
Em7/A
Am7
- cial, spe - cial.
Some - one,
Em7/A
Am7
Am7/D
Dm7
Am7/D
Dm7
some- one. I'll
Fmaj7/G
G9
Fmaj7/G
G9
Repeat ad lib. and Fade
give it to some - one, I'll give it to some - one spe -

MERRY CHRISTMAS, DARLING

Words and Music by RICHARD CARPENTER
and FRANK POOLER

Rubato
Cm7
3 fr
Dm7
Gm7
3 fr
Cm7
3 fr
F7
B♭
Greet-ing cards have all been sent, the Christ-mas rush is through,
Gm
3 fr
G♭+
B♭/F
C/E
Cm7
3 fr
Moderately slow
F
but I still have one wish to make, a spe-cial one for you;
B♭maj9
Cm/B♭
B♭maj9
Fm7
B♭9sus
4 fr
mer - ry Christ - mas, dar - ling. We're a - part, that's true; but

Eb
F/Eb
Dm7
Gm7
Cm7
Dm
Eb6
Eb/F
F7
I can dream and in my dreams, I'm Christ - mas-ing with you.
Bbmaj9
Cm/Bb
Bbmaj9
Fm7
Bb9
Hol - i - days are joy - ful, there's al - ways some - thing new. But
Eb
F/Eb
Dm7
Gm7
C/E
Ebm6
Ab7
ev - 'ry day's a hol - i - day when I'm near to you. The
Db
Eb/Db
Cm7
Fm
Bbm7
Eb7
Ab
lights on my tree I wish you could see, I wish it ev - 'ry day. The

Fm
Fm(maj7)
Fm7
F7
B♭
Cm
Dm
Cm7
F
logs on the fire fill me with de-sire to see you and to ___ say that I
B♭maj9
Cm/B♭
B♭maj9
Fm7
E7♭5
wish you mer - ry Christ-mas, hap-py New Year too. I've
To Coda
E♭
F/E♭
Dm7
Gm7
Cm7
F7
B♭
A♭7
D.S. al Coda
just one wish on this Christ-mas Eve; I wish I were with you. The ___
CODA
Cm
F
E♭
Dm7♭5
G7
Cm7
F7
B♭
I wish I were with you, I wish I were with you. ___
rit.

LET IT SNOW! LET IT SNOW! LET IT SNOW!

Words by SAMMY CAHN
Music by JULE STYNE

Moderately
A♭dim7
C7
F
C7
F
mf
Oh, the weath-er out - side is fright - ful, but the
F/A
A♭dim7
C7/G
D7/F♯
Gm
D7
Gm
A♭dim7
fire is so de - light - ful, and since we've no place to go, let it
C7
F
F
C7
F
snow! let it snow! let it snow! It does - n't show signs of stop - ping, and I
fi - re is slow - ly dy - ing and, my

F/A
A♭dim7
C7/G
D7/F♯
Gm
D7
Gm
A♭dim7
brought some corn for pop - ping. The lights are turned way down low;
dear, we're still good - bye - ing, but as long as you love me so,
let it
C7
To Coda
F
C
C♯dim7
snow! let it snow! let it snow! When we fi - nal-ly kiss good - night, how I'll
Dm7
G7
C
B+
Gm/B♭
A7
hate go - ing out in the storm! But if you'll real - ly hold me tight,
D7
G7
C7
D.S. al Coda
CODA
F
all the way home I'll be warm. The
snow!

THE LITTLE BOY THAT SANTA CLAUS FORGOT

Words and Music by MICHAEL CARR,
TOMMY CONNOR and JIMMY LEACH

Slowly
F Fdim7 F Gm7 D♭7 C7
mf
F Fdim7 F Gm7
Christ - mas comes but once a year for ev - 'ry girl and boy, the
G9 C7 Fmaj9 F6
laugh - ter and the joy they find in each new toy. I'll
F Fdim7 F Gm7 B♭m F
tell you of a lit - tle boy who lives a - cross the way; this

G9
D♭7
4fr
C7
lit - tle fel - ler's Christ - mas is just an - oth - er day. He's the
F
Am7♭5
D7
G7
lit - tle boy that San - ta Claus for - got,
3
Gm7
C7
Gm7♭5
5fr
and good - ness knows he did - n't want a
F
F6
F/A
lot. He sent a note to

A♭dim7
4fr
Gm7
C
San - ta for some sol - diers and a drum; it
3
Gm7
Gm7♭5
5fr
C7
F
F♯dim7
broke his lit - tle heart when he found San - ta had - n't
Gm7
C7
F
Am7♭5
D7
come. In the street he en - vies all those luck - y
G7
Gm7
C7
boys, then wan - ders home to
3
3

Gm7
A7
Dm
F7
last year's bro - ken toys.
I'm so
B♭
Gm7♭5
5fr
F
C7/G
G♯dim7
F/A
sor - ry for that lad - die, he has - n't got a
D7
Gm7
C7
G9
C7♭9
dad - dy, the lit - tle boy that San - ta Claus for -
1
F
F♯dim7
Gm7
C7
2
F
D♭9
F6
got.
He's the
got.

LITTLE SAINT NICK

Words and Music by BRIAN WILSON
and MIKE LOVE

Moderately fast
G
C/E
G/D
C/E
mf
Am7
D7
Ooh,
Mer - ry Christ - mas, Saint
G
Nick.
(Christ - mas comes this time each year.)
Am7
Ooh.
D7
Well,
way up north where the
lit - tle bob - sled, we call it
haul - in' through the snow at a

Original key: G♭ major. This edition has been transposed up one half-step to be more playable.

Am7
D7
G
Gmaj7
air gets cold, there's a tale a - bout Christ - mas that you've
Old Saint Nick, but she'll walk a to - bog - gan with a
fright - 'nin' speed with a half a doz - en deer with
G6
G♯dim7
Am7
D7
all been told. And a real fa - mous cat all dressed
four speed stick. She's can - dy ap - ple red with a
Ru - dy to lead. He's got - ta wear his gog - gles 'cause the
Am7
D7
G
Gmaj7
up in red, and he spends the whole year work - in'
ski for a wheel, and when San - ta hits the gas, man, just
snow real - ly flies, and he's cruis - in' ev - 'ry pad with a
G6
G7
C
out on his sled.
watch her peel.
lit - tle sur - prise.
It's the Lit - tle Saint Nick. (Lit - tle

To Coda
Am7
Saint Nick.) It's the Lit - tle Saint Nick. (Lit - tle
1
D
Saint Nick.) Just a
2
D
Saint Nick.)
C
F/C
C
Run, run, rein - deer.
F
B♭/F
F
Run, run, rein - deer.
Oh.

C
F/C
C
Run, run, rein - deer.
A
N.C.
D.S. al Coda
Run, run, rein - deer. He don't miss no one. And
CODA
G
E7/G#
Am7
D7
Lit - tle Saint Nick. (Lit - tle Saint Nick.) Ah,
Am7
D7
Repeat and Fade
G
E7/G#
Optional Ending
G
Mer - ry Christ - mas, Saint Nick. Ah, Nick.
(Christ - mas comes this time each year.)

LO, HOW A ROSE E'ER BLOOMING

15th Century German Carol
Translated by THEODORE BAKER
Music from *Alte Catholische Geistliche Kirchengesäng*

In a traditional style
G C G D
Lo, How A Rose E'er Bloom -
Em C G D Am/E Em G/D D7 G
ing From ten - der stem hath sprung! Of Jes - se's
C G D Em C G D Am/E Em G/D D7 G
lin - eage com - ing As men of old have sung.
Am Bm Em/G A7 D D7/F# G C G D
It came, a flow'r - et bright, A - mid the cold of win -

E Am D7/A G/B Am D7 G/D D7sus D7 G
ter, When half spent was the night. I - sa - iah
C G D Em C G/D D Am/E Em G/D D7 G
'twas fore told it, The Rose I have in mind,
C G D Em C G/D D Am/E Em
With Ma - ry we be - hold it, The Vir - gin Moth -
G/D D7 G Am Bm Em/G A7 D D7/F# G
- er kind. To show God's love a - right. She bore to
C G D E Am D7/A G/B Am D7 G/D D7sus D7 G
men a Sav - iour, When half spent was the night.

A MARSHMALLOW WORLD

Words by CARL SIGMAN
Music by PETER DE ROSE
Brightly
mf
C C/B Am7 C/G C Am7
It's A Marsh - mal - low World in the win - ter When the snow comes to cov - er the
Marsh - mal - low clouds be - ing friend - ly In the arms of the ev - er - green
G7 Dm7 G7 C Am7
ground. It's the time for play It's a whipped cream day
trees. And the sun is red Like a pump - kin head It's
1 Bm/F# Am/E Bdim/D Am/C
I wait for it the whole year
Gsus G7
round. Those are
2 Bm/F# Am/E Dm G7 C6 Gm7 C7
shin - ing so your nose won't freeze. The world is your snow - ball;

F Dm Gm7 C9 C7 F Dm7 Am7 D7
See how it grows. That's how it goes, When - ev - er it snows. The world is your snow - ball:
G Em Am7 D7 Gsus G7 C C/B
Just for a song, Get out and roll it a - long. It's a yum - yum - my world made for
Am7 C/G C Am7 G7 Dm7 G7
sweet - hearts Take a walk with your fa - vor - ite girl. It's a su - gar date What if
To Coda
Am7 D7 Dm/G C/G Dm/G G7 C6
D.S. al Coda
(with repeat)
spring is late. In win - ter It's A Marsh - mal - low World. It's a
Coda C6
World.

MERRY CHRISTMAS, BABY

Words and Music by LOU BAXTER
and JOHNNY MOORE

Slow Blues
G7
C7
G7
Instrumental solo ad lib. (2nd time only)
mf
C7
G7
D7
C7
G7

C7
Mer-ry, mer-ry Christ-mas, ba - by,
sure did treat me nice.
G7
I said mer - ry
C7
Christ-mas, ba - by,
sure did treat me nice.
G7
Gave me a dia -

D7
C7
mond ring for Christ - mas,
now I'm liv - ing in par - a - dise.
G7
Well, I'm
G7
C7
feel - ing might - y fine;
got good mu - sic on my ra - di - o.
G7
Well I'm feel -

C7
ing might-y fine; got good mu-sic on my ra-di-o.
G7
Well, I wan-
D7
C7
To Coda
-na kiss you, ba-by while you're stand-ing 'neath the mis-tle-toe.
1
D7

2
G
C/D
G
D7
D.S. al Coda
Well, I'm
CODA
G7
D7#9
I said mer -
G7
C7
- ry Christ-mas, ba - by,
yes, you sure did treat me nice._
G7
Mer-ry,

C7
mer-ry Christ-mas, ba-by,
well, you sure did treat me nice.
Gave me a dia-mond
D7
Db7
C7
ring for Christ-mas,
now I'm liv-ing in par-a-dise.
Repeat ad lib. and Fade
Optional Ending
G7
G7/D
I said mer-

MERRY CHRISTMAS FROM THE FAMILY

Words and Music by
ROBERT EARL KEEN

Moderately
G
Csus2
G
Mom got drunk and
mf
Csus2
G
Csus2
Dad got drunk at our Christ - mas par - ty.
G
G/F#
Em
C
D
We were drink - in' cham - pagne punch and home - made egg - nog.

G
C
G
Lit - tle sis - ter brought her new boy - friend.
He was a
Csus2
G
G/F#
Em
Mex - i - can.
We did - n't know what to think of him till he
C
D
G
sang, "Fe - liz Na - vi - dad, Fe - liz Na - vi - dad."
Csus2
G
C

G
C
G
Broth - er Ken brought his kids with him, the three from his
C
G
G/F#
Em
C
first wife Lynn, and the two i - den - ti - cal twins from his sec - ond wife Mar - y
D
G
Csus2
Nell. 'Course he brought his new wife Kaye,
G
C
G
G/F#
Em
who talks all a - bout A A, chain smok - in' while the ster - e - o plays,

C
D
G
"No - el, No - el, the first No - el."
C(add2)
G
C(add2)
D
C
Carve the tur - key, turn the ball game on, mix mar - ga - ri - tas when the
Carve the tur - key, turn the ball game on, make blood - y mar - ys 'cause we
egg - nog's gone.
all want one.
D
Send some - bod - y to the Quik - Pak store.
Send some - bod - y to the Stop 'n' Go.

C D

We need some ice and an ex - ten - sion chord, a can of bean dip and some
We need some cel - 'ry and a can of fake snow, a bag of lem - ons and some

C

Di - et Rites, a box of tam - pons and some Marl - bo - ro Lights.
Di - et Sprites, a box of tam - pons and some Sa - lem Lights.

G G/F# Em C To Coda

Hal - le - lu - jah, ev - 'ry - bod - y say "cheese." Mer - ry Christ - mas from the

D G C(add2) G

fam - i - ly.

Csus2
G
Csus2
Fran and Ri - ta drove from Har - lin - gen.
G
C
G
G/F♯
I can't re - mem - ber how I'm kin to them.
But when they tried to plug their
Em
C
D
mo - tor home in, they blew our Christ - mas lights.
3
G
Csus2
G
Cous - in Da - vid knew just what went wrong,
so we all wait - ed out on

Csus2
G
G/F#
Em
our front lawn. _ He threw the break - er and the lights came on _ and we
C
D
G
C(add2)
sang, "Si - lent night, oh, _ si - lent night." _
G
C
D.S. al Coda
CODA
D
G
fam - i - ly. _
C(add2)
G
C(add2)
G
Fe - liz Na - vi - dad.
rit.

MERRY MERRY CHRISTMAS, BABY

Words and Music by MARGO SYLVIA
and GIL LOPEZ

Slow Fifties Rock
mf
8va
2
Mer - ry, mer - ry Christ - mas
E♭
E♭dim
ba - by.
Al - though you're with some - bod - y
F7
B♭
new,
thought I'd send a card to

Fm
Fm7
B♭7-9
say that I wish this hol - i - day would find me be -
E♭
Edim
B♭7
no chord
side you.
Mer - ry, mer - ry Christ - mas
E♭
E♭dim
E♭
ba - by.
Instrumental on repeat
And a hap - py New Year
F7
B♭
too
It was Christ - mas Eve we

Fm
Fm7
Bb7
met a hol - i - day I can't for - get, 'cause that's when we fell in
Eb
Abm
Eb
Eb+
love.
Instrumental ends
I still re -
Ab
mem - ber
the gifts we gave to each
Eb
oth - er.
This love I

F
hold
With - in my heart
B♭7
Fm7
B♭7
n.c.
Still
grows though, we're
a - part.
Have a Mer - ry, Christ - mas
E♭
E♭dim
E♭
3-
3-
ba - by.
And a Hap - py New Year
F7
B♭
too
am hop - ing that you'll

1
Fm
Fm7
Bb7-9
find A love as true as mine Mer - ry, mer - ry Christ - mas
Eb
Abm
Eb
Bb6
Fm7/Bb
ba - by.
2
Fm
Fm7
Bb7-9
find a love as true as mine. Mer - ry, mer - ry Christ-mas,
Bb9
Eb6
Fm7
Emaj7 Ebmaj7
ba - by.

THE MERRY CHRISTMAS POLKA

Words by PAUL FRANCIS WEBSTER
Music by SONNY BURKE

Moderately (Tempo di Polka)
f
mf
mp
Bb
Cm7
F7
They're tun - ing up the fid - dles now, the fid - dles now, the
Eb
F
C7
fid - dles now, There's wine to warm the mid - dles now and set your head a -
whirl. A - round and round the room we go, the room we go, the

Eb Bb F C F7
room we go. A - round and round the room we go, So get your - self a
Bb Bb
girl.
f
mf
F7 Eb Bb
Now ev - 'ry heart will start to tin - gle,
Eb Fdim F7 Bb
When sleigh bells jin - gle on San - ta's sleigh,
Bbdim F7 Eb Bb
To - geth - er we will greet Kris Krin - gle.

F7 Gb7 Cm7 F7 Bb7
And an - oth - er Christ - mas Day.
Brightly
Eb
Come on and dance The Mer - ry Christ - mas
dance The Mer - ry Christ - mas
mf-f
Ab
Pol - ka, Let ev - 'ry one be hap - py and
Pol - ka, Let ev - 'ry la - dy step with her
Eb Bb7 Eb7 Ab Bb7
gay, Oh! it's the time to be jol - ly and
beau A - round a tree to the ceil - ing with
Eb Cm Fm Gm Fm Am7-5
deck the halls with hol - ly, So let's have a jol - ly hol - i -
lots of time for steal - ing, Those kiss - es be - neath the mis - tle-

Bb7
F7-5
Bb7
Eb
day! Come on and dance The Mer - ry Christ - mas
toe! Come on and dance The Mer - ry Christ - mas
Ab
Pol - ka, An - oth - er joy - ous sea - son has be -
Pol - ka, With ev - 'ry bod - y join - ing in the
G
G7
F#7
G7
Fm7
Bb7
gun, Roll out the yule - tide bar - rels and
fun, Roll out the bar - rels that cheer you and
Gm7
Cm
Fm7
Bbdim
Fm
Eb
Bb7
sing out the car - ols,
shout 'til they hear you,
A Mer - ry Christ - mas ev - 'ry
Eb
Bbdim
Bb7
Eb
Ab6
Eb
one! Come on and one!

MISS YOU MOST AT CHRISTMAS TIME

Words and Music by MARIAH CAREY
and WALTER AFANASIEFF

With feeling
D
Gm6/D
D
Woo;
p
With pedal
Gm6/D
D
The fire is burn - ing, the
gaze out the win - dow this
mp - mf
Gm6/D
D
room's all a - glow,
out - side the De - cem - ber wind
cold win - ter's night
at all of the twin - kl - ing

Gm6/D
D
blows. A - way in the dis - tance the
lights, a - lone in the dark - ness, re -
C#m7b5
2fr
F#7#5
Bm
Bb7
car - ol - ers sing in the snow.
mem - ber - ing when you were mine.
Am11
5fr
D7sus
D7
G
Ev - 'ry - bod - y's laugh - ing, the
Ev - 'ry - bod - y's smil - ing, the
D/F#
B7
Em7
world is cel - e - brat - ing and ev - 'ry - one's so hap - py ex -
whole world is re - joic - ing and ev - 'ry - one's em - brac - ing ex -

Em7/A
Gm6/A
D
cept for me to - night. Be - cause
cept for you and I. Ba - by
I miss you
F#7sus
F#7#5
Bm
most at Christ-mas time and I can't get you,
Am7/D
D7
G
get you off my mind.
Ev - 'ry oth - er sea - son comes a -
F#m7
F#/A#
Bm
Bm7/E
E9♭5
E9
long and I'm al - right.
But then I miss you

Em9
F#m7
G
A7♭9
6fr
1
D
Gm6/D
most at Christ - mas time.
Ooh,
D
Gm6/D
2
D
yeah;
I
cresc.
F#7sus
F#7
Oh;
In the spring - time those
f
Bm
Gm/B♭
A7sus
A7
mem - 'ries start to fade
with the A - pril

Dmaj7
F#7sus
F#7
rain.
Through the sum-mer days, till
A#dim7
Bm7
2fr
E7sus
E7
aut - umn's leaves are gone,
I get by with - out you till the
Gmaj7/A
Gm7/C
F
snow be-gins to fall and then I miss you
A7sus
A7
Dm7
most at Christ-mas time and I can't get you, no-no-no no,

Cm7
3 fr
Cm7/F
F7
B♭maj7
get you off my mind.
Ev - 'ry oth - er sea - son comes a -
A7sus
A7
Dm7
G9
Gm7
3fr
long and I'm al - right.
But then I miss you
molto rit.
p
Am7
B♭
C7♭9
F
most at Christ - mas time.
B♭m6/F
F
Fmaj7
B♭/F
B♭m/F
F
Ooh.

O CHRISTMAS TREE

Traditional German Carol

Moderately
F
F/E
Cm6/E♭
D7sus
D7
Gm
D7
Gm
C7
Fsus
F
O
mf
Fsus
F
C/B♭
A7
Dm
Gm
D
Gm
C7
C7/F
F
Christ - mas tree! O Christ - mas tree, you stand in ver - dant beau - ty! O
Christ - mas tree! O Christ - mas tree, much plea - sure doth thou bring me! O
Christ - mas tree! O Christ - mas tree, thy can - dles shine out bright - ly! O
B♭
F/A
C7
F
F♯dim
Gm
C7
Fsus
F
Christ - mas tree, O Christ - mas tree, you stand in ver - dant beau - ty! Your
Christ - mas tree, O Christ - mas tree, much plea - sure doth thou bring me! For
Christ - mas tree, O Christ - mas tree, thy can - dles shine out bright - ly! Each

Fmaj7
D7♭9
D9
Gm
C9
B♭dim7
F
C
boughs are green in sum - mer's glow, and do not fade in win - ter's snow. O
ev - 'ry year the Christ - mas tree brings to us all both joy and glee. O
bough doth hold its ti - ny light that makes each toy to spark - le bright. O
F
Gm/C
C/B♭
A
D7
Gm
D
Gm
C7
1,2
B♭dim7
F
Christ - mas tree, O Christ - mas tree, you stand in ver - dant beau - ty! O
Christ - mas tree, O Christ - mas tree, much plea - sure doth thou bring me! O
Christ - mas tree, O Christ - mas tree, thy can - dles shine out
3
B♭dim7
F
C
F
F/E
Cm6/E♭
D7sus
D7
Gm
D7
Gm
C7
C7/F
F
bright - ly! O Christ - mas tree, O Christ - mas tree, thy can - dles shine out bright - ly!

O COME, ALL YE FAITHFUL
(Adeste Fideles)

Words and Music by JOHN FRANCIS WADE
Latin Words translated by FREDERICK OAKELEY

Triumphantly
f
G
D
O Come, All Ye Faith - ful,
Sing choirs of an - gels,
G D G C G/D D Em D A
joy - ful and tri - um - phant, O come ye, O
sing in ex - ul - ta - tion, O sing all ye
D A7 D G D/A A7 D
come ye to Beth - le - hem;
ci - ti - zens of heav - en a - bove.

G D7 G D7sus D7 G D Em Am
Come and be - hold him, born the King of
Glo - ry to God in the
D G D G D7 G
an - gels;
high - est
O come, let us a - dore him, O
D G D7 G D G D7 G D A7
come, let us a - dore him, O come, let us a -
D D7 G C G/D D7 G
dore him, Christ, the Lord!

O COME, O COME IMMANUEL

Plainsong, 13th Century
Words translated by JOHN M. NEALE and HENRY S. COFFIN

Like an old plainsong

mf

O

Guitar tacet

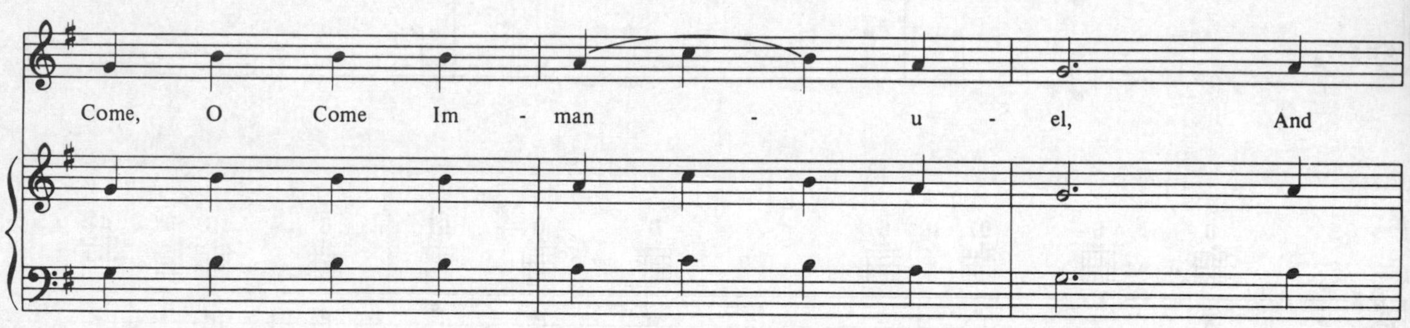
Come, O Come Im - man - u - el, And

ran - som cap - tive Is - ra - el, That mourns in lone - ly

ex - ile here Un - til the Son of God ap -
G
D
Em
Bm
G
C
D
pear. Re - joice, re - joice! Im - man - u -
Em
D
G
C
G/B
Am
Em/B
Bm
Em
el shall come to Thee, O Is - ra - el! O
Am
Em
G
C
come, Thou key of Dav - id, come And o - pen wide our

Am
Em
Bm
Em
Am
Em/B
B
Em
D/A
A7
heav'n - ly home. Make safe the way that leads on
D
Em
D
Bm
G
Am
G/D
D7
G
high And close the path to mis - er - y. Re -
D
Em
Bm
G
C
D
Em
D
joice, re - joice! Im - man - u - el shall
G
C
G
Am
Em
Bm
Em
come to Thee, O Is - ra - el!

O LITTLE TOWN OF BETHLEHEM

Words by PHILLIPS BROOKS
Music by LEWIS H. REDNER

Quietly
mp
F Fdim F
O Lit - tle Town Of
For Christ is born of
F#dim Gm F/C C7 F F7 D Gm
Beth - le - hem, How still we see thee lie! A - bove thy deep and dream - less sleep The
Ma - y, And gath - ered all a - bove, While mor - tals sleep the an - gels keep Their
F/C C7 F C7/G G#dim A Dm Gm
si - lent stars go by; Yet in thy dark streets shin - eth The ev - er - last - ing
watch of won - d'ring love. O morn - ing stars, to - geth - er Pro - claim the ho - ly
A F Fdim F F#dim Gm Bdim F/C C7 F
light; The hopes and fears of all the years Are met in thee to - night.
birth! And prais - es sing to God the King, And peace to men on earth!

O HOLY NIGHT

French Words by PLACIDE CAPPEAU
English Words by JOHN S. DWIGHT
Music by ADOLPHE ADAM

Slow and flowing
C
C/E
mp
O ho - ly night, the
Tru - ly He taught us to
F
C
stars are bright - ly shin - ing; it is the night of the
love one an - oth - er; His law is love, and His
G
C
dear Sav - ior's birth. Long lay the
gos - pel is peace. Chains shall He

C/E
F
C
C7
world in sin and er - ror pin - ing, till He ap -
break, for the slave is our broth - er, and in His
Em/B
B7
Em
peared and the soul felt its worth. A
name all op - pres - sion shall cease. Sweet
G7
C
thrill of hope the wea - ry soul re - joic - es, for
hymns of joy in grate - ful cho - rus raise we, let
G7
C
yon - der breaks a new and glor - ious morn.
all with - in us praise His ho - ly name.

Am
Em
Fall on your knees, oh,
Christ is the Lord, oh,
Dm
Am
hear the an - gel voic - es! O
praise His name for - ev - er! His
C
G/F
C/E
F
night di - vine, o
pow'r and glo - ry
C/G
G7
C
night when Christ was born! O
ev - er - more pro - claim! His
cresc.

1
G
G/F
C/E
F
night, O ho - ly
f
C/G
G7
C
night, O night di - vine!
decresc.
2
G
G/F
C/E
F
pow'r and glo - ry
f
C/G
G7
C
ev - er - more pro - claim!
decresc.
rit.
p

OLD TOY TRAINS

Words and Music by
ROGER MILLER

Moderately
F
Gm7/F
F
Gm7/F
F
Gm7/F
mp
F
C7/E
Old toy trains, little toy tracks, little toy drums
Bb/D
C
F
F7
coming from a sack, carried by a man dressed in white and
Bb
F
C7
F
red. Little boy don't you think it's time you were in bed? Close your

C7 Bb

eyes, listen to the skies.

F Dm G7

All is calm, all is well; soon you'll hear Kris

C/E Dm7 C7 F

Krin - gle and the jin - gle bell bring - in' Old toy trains, lit - tle toy tracks,

C/E Bb/D C

lit - tle toy drums com - in' from a sack, car - ried by a

F
F7
B♭
F
C7
man dressed in white and red. Lit - tle boy don't you think it's time you were in
1
F
Gm7/F
F
Gm7/F
F
Gm7/F
bed?
F
So close your bed?
2
F
C7
Lit - tle boy don't you think it's time you were in
F
Gm7/F
F
Gm7/F
F
bed?
rit.

ONE BRIGHT STAR

Words and Music by
JOHN JARVIS

Flowing
G
D/G
G
D/F#
Em7
C
p
G
D
C/E
D/F#
G
D/G
G
D/G
D
G
D/G
G
D/F#
Long long_ a - go in a
Em7
C
G
D
world dark_ and cold a night so still win-ters

C
G/D
Dsus
D
chill one bright star was shin - ing. On a
G
D/G
G
D/F#
Em7
C
bed made of hay in a man - ger he
G
Am
Em
D
C
lay. The shep-herds came they knew his name
G/D
Dsus
D/F#
G
C
king of kings. A brand new day they saw the light in the

D/F#
G
C/E
D/F#
G
dark - ness. It shines on love and ten - der - ness
C
D/F#
G
G/A
Am
brings out the hope that's in all of us. May it shine its light on
G/D
D7
G/D
D7
G
D/G
G
D/F#
Em7
C
you this Christ-mas night.
G
D
C/E
D/F#
Gsus
G

Gsus
G
A
E/A
A
E/G#
F#m7
D
On this Christ - mas day may that star - light your
A
Bm
F#m
E
D
A/E
way this Christ-mas eve. I still be - lieve that same star still
Esus
E/G#
A
D
E/G#
A
shines on me. I saw the light in the dark - ness it
D/F#
E/G#
A
D
shines on love and ten - der - ness brings out the hope that's in

E/G#
A
A/B
Bm
A/E
E7
A/E
E7
all of us. May it shine its light on you this Christ - mas
A
E/A
A
A/B
Bm
A/E
E7
A/E
E7
night. May it shine its light on you this Christ-mas
rit.
A
E/A
A
E/G#
F#m7
D
A
night.
a tempo
E
D/F#
E/G#
A
Asus
D/E
A
rit.

PLEASE COME HOME FOR CHRISTMAS

Words and Music by CHARLES BROWN
and GENE REDD

Moderately
A6
A
Bells will be ring - ing
sing - ing
mf
Amaj7
A7
the sad, sad news,
"Si - lent Night",
oh what a
Christ-mas
D
D#dim7
Christ - mas to have the blues!
car - ols by can - dle - light.

A
D
My ba - by's gone,
I have no
Please come home for Christ-mas,
please come home for
A
A/G#
F#m7
B7
friends
to wish me greet-ings
Christ-mas;
if not for Christ-mas,
1
E7
E7#5
once a - gain.
Choirs will be
2
E7
A
A7
by New Year's night.
Friends and re -

D
Dm
la - tions
send sal - u - ta - tions
A
E7#5
sure
as the stars
shine a - bove.
A
A7
D
For this is Christ - mas,
Dm
yes, Christ - mas my
dear,
it's the time of

B7
E7
year to be with the one you love.
E7#5
A
Amaj7
So won't you tell me you'll never-more
(Instrumental)
A7
D
roam. Christ-mas and New Year
D#dim
will find you home.
(Instrumental ends)
Ooo
There'll be no more

A
C♯7
F♯m
A/E
sor - row
no grief
and pain
D
B7/D♯
A/E
F♯m7
1
B7
E7
and I'll be
hap - py,
hap - py.
hap - py
once a -
A
E7♯5
2
B7
E7
gain.
Christ - mas
once a -
A
D/A
A
gain.

PRETTY PAPER

Words and Music by
WILLIE NELSON

Slowly, with expression
mf
mp
G
D7
G
Crowd-ed streets, bus - y feet hus - tle by him.
Down-town
D7
G
shop - pers, Christ - mas is night.
There he sits all a -
G7
C
A7
lone on the side - walk.
Hop - ing that you won't pass him

D7
G
D7
G
by.
Should you stop;
Bet - ter
not,
much too
bus - y.
D7
G
You're in a
hur - ry,
my
how
time
does
fly.
In the
G7
C
G
dis - tance
the
ring - ing
of
laugh - ter
And in the
midst
of the
D7
G
laugh - ter
he
cries.
Pret - ty
pa - per,
pret - ty
rib - bons
of

D7
blue.
Wrap your pres - ents to your dar - ling from
G
G7
C
you.
Pret - ty pen - cils to write, "I love you."
G
D7
1 C
G
Pret - ty pa - per, pret - ty rib - bons of blue.
Pret - ty
mf
2 G
blue.
decresc.
rit.
pp

ROCKIN' AROUND THE CHRISTMAS TREE

Music and Lyrics by
JOHNNY MARKS

Moderate Shuffle
C
Am
Dm
G7
mf
C
G7
Rock - in' a - round the Christ - mas tree at the Christ - mas par - ty hop.
Mis - tle - toe hung where you can see ev - 'ry
C
cou - ple tries to stop. Rock - in' a - round the

G7
Christ - mas tree, let the Christ - mas spir - it ring.
Lat - er we'll have some pun - kin pie and we'll do some car - ol -
C
F
G♯dim
F
G♯dim
F
Em
ing. You will get a sen - ti - men - tal feel - ing when you
Am
Am(maj7)
Am7
D7
hear voic - es sing - ing, "Let's be jol - ly, deck the halls with

G7
C
boughs of hol - ly." Rock - in' a - round the Christ - mas tree, have a
G7
hap - py hol - i - day.
Ev - 'ry - one danc - ing mer - ri - ly in the
1
Dm7/G
G7
C
new old fash - ioned way.
2
Dm7/G
G7
new old fash - ioned
C
way.
sfz

SHARE LOVE

Words and Music by
NATHAN MORRIS

Moderately
N.C.
G#m7
F#/A#
Amaj7/B
F#/G#
Amaj7/B
It's that
mf
E
G#+
B/C#
C#m7
time of the year a - gain for you to share all the
fam - 'lies all a - round, chil - dren are hap - py with what they found,
Cmaj9
Bm7
Am7
F(add9)
love that you have with ev - 'ry wom - an and ev - 'ry man, to share love.
giv - ing things on this day and thank - ing our God, for teach - ing us the way to share love.

E
N.C.
As the
E
G#+
B/C#
C#m7
4fr
Christ-mas Day is here and the Lord has brought us near to share
snow is fall-ing down, pre-sents un-wrapped un-der-neath the tree bring-ing
Cmaj7
Bm7
2fr
Am7
love with your fam-i-ly and thank God for al-low-ing you to see that
tid-ings of great joy to ev-'ry lit-tle girl and boy. You know
E
B/C#
C#m7
4fr
Christ-mas is the time to share with the one you

Cmaj7
D
Cmaj7
Bm7
2fr
love. Share good things, joy, and glad tid - ings. Share love.
E
B/C#
C#m7
4fr
Giv - ing all you have this day lets the world
Cmaj7
D
Cmaj7
D
know that you care and you will be there to share love.
1
E

2
E
Emaj7
Dmaj7
Now, the true
Cmaj7
Am7
G
mean-ing of Christ-mas is fall-ing on your knees and thank-ing the Lord
Am7
Cmaj7
Am7
Bm7
2fr
Cmaj7
D9sus
for what He's done, giv-ing the world His on-ly Son.
N.C.
Am7
N.C.
Oh, ooh, let Him

E
B/C#
C#m7
4fr
in.
Christ - mas is the time to share with the one you
Cmaj7
D
Cmaj7
Bm7
2fr
love. Share good things, joy, and glad tid - ings. Share love.
E
B/C#
C#m7
4fr
Giv - ing all you have this day lets the world
Cmaj7
D
Cmaj7
D
Repeat ad lib. and Fade
know that you care and you will be there to share love.

RUDOLPH THE RED-NOSED REINDEER

Music and Lyrics by
JOHNNY MARKS

Moderately fast
G/B
F/A
Em/G
Dm/F
C/E
B/D♯
4 fr
mf
mp
rit.
Dm
G7
Dm7
Em
G9
C
You know Dash - er and Danc - er and Pranc - er and Vix - en,
p
mf ad lib.
smoothly
Dm7
Em
G9
C
Am
E7/B
Com - et and Cu - pid and Don - ner and Blitz - en, but do you re -
Am/C
Am7
D9
4 fr
G7
call the most fa - mous rein - deer of all?

C
C/E
E♭dim7
Ru - dolph The Red - Nosed Rein - deer had a ver - y shin - y
a tempo
lightly
G7
nose, and if you ev - er saw it,
G7♯5
C
you would e - ven say it glows. All of the oth - er
C/E
E♭dim7
G7
rein - deer used to laugh and call him names.

They nev - er let poor Ru - dolph join in an - y rein - deer
C
C7
F
C
Cmaj7
games. Then one fog - gy Christ - mas Eve,
Dm
G7
C
C#dim7
G/D
San - ta came to say, "Ru - dolph, with your
Gmaj7
G#dim7
Am7
D7
G7
nose so bright, won't you guide my sleigh to - night?"_

C
C/E
E♭dim7
Then how the rein - deer loved him, as they shout - ed out with
G7
glee: "Ru - dolph The Red - Nosed Rein - deer,
1
C
G9
G7♭9
4fr
2
G7/D
C♯dim7
you'll go down in his - to - ry!" you'll go down in
G7/D
G7
C
Dm7
G7
C
his - to - ry!"

SILENT NIGHT

Words by JOSEPH MOHR
Translated by JOHN F. YOUNG
Music by FRANZ X. GRUBER
Quietly
F7
B♭
B♭/F
mp
F7
B♭
B♭
Si - lent night, ho - ly night! All is calm, all is bright.
Si - lent night, ho - ly night! Shep - herds quake at the sight.
Si - lent night, ho - ly night! Son of God love's pure light.
F7
B♭
E♭
3
B♭
Round yon Vir - gin Moth - er and Child.
Glo - ries stream from heav - en a - far,
Ra - diant beams from Thy ho - ly face

E♭
B♭
F7
Ho - ly In - fant so ten - der and mild, Sleep in
Heaven - ly hosts sing Al - le - lu - ia, Christ the
With the dawn of re - deem - ing grace, Je - sus
B♭
B♭/F
heav - en - ly peace, Sleep in
Sav - ior is born! Christ the
Lord at Thy birth. Je - sus
F7
1,2
B♭
3
B♭
heav - en - ly peace.
Sav - ior is born.
Lord at Thy birth.

SILVER BELLS

from the Paramount Picture THE LEMON DROP KID

Words and Music by JAY LIVINGSTON
and RAY EVANS

Moderately

Bb F/A Dm/F Bb F/A Dm/F Cm/Eb Bb/D Eb

8va

f *mf* *rall.*

F7sus F7 Bb Cm7

mp
a tempo

Christ - mas makes you feel e -

F7 Bb Cm7

mo - tion - al. It may bring par - ties or thoughts de -

F7 Gm Gm(maj7) Gm7

vo - tion - al. What - ev - er hap - pens or what may

mf

C7 B♭/D D♭dim7 F7/C C7♭9
3fr
be, here is what Christ - mas - time means to
mp
rall.
Cm7/F F7 B♭ B♭maj7 B♭7 E♭
3fr
me. Cit - y side - walks, bus - y side - walks dressed in hol - i - day
street lights, e - ven stop - lights blink a bright red and
E♭6 F7 B♭
style; in the air there's a feel - ing of Christ - mas.
green as the shop - pers rush home with their treas - ures.
E♭ B♭/D Cm7/F B♭ B♭maj7 B♭7
3fr
Chil - dren laugh - ing, peo - ple pass - ing, meet - ing
Hear the snow crunch, see the kids bunch, this is

E♭
3fr
E♭6
F7
smile af - ter smile, and on ev - 'ry street cor - ner you
San - ta's big scene, and a - bove all this bus - tle you
B♭
hear:
hear:
Sil - ver bells,
E♭
3fr
F
C7
sil - ver bells, it's Christ - mas -
F7
B♭
time in the cit - y.

B♭
E♭
3 fr
Ring - a - ling,
hear them ring,
F
C7
F7
soon it will be Christ - mas
1
B♭
E♭/B♭
6fr
B♭maj7
Cm/B♭
F7(add13)
Day.
Strings of
2
B♭
E♭/B♭
6fr
B♭maj7
F7
B♭
Day.
rall.

SING WE NOW OF CHRISTMAS

Joyfully

Traditional

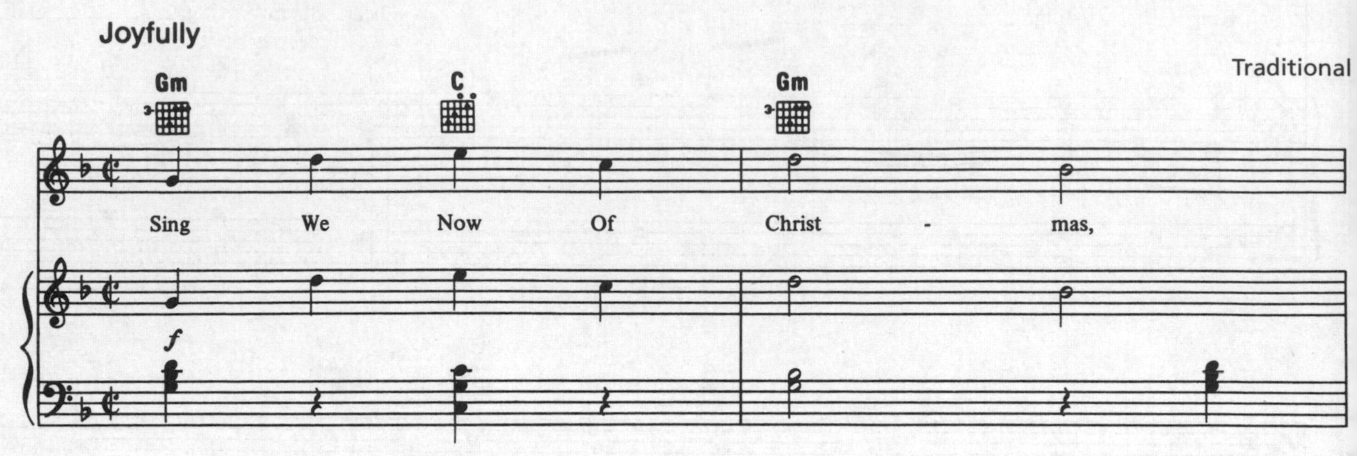
Gm
C
Gm
Sing We Now Of Christ - mas,
f

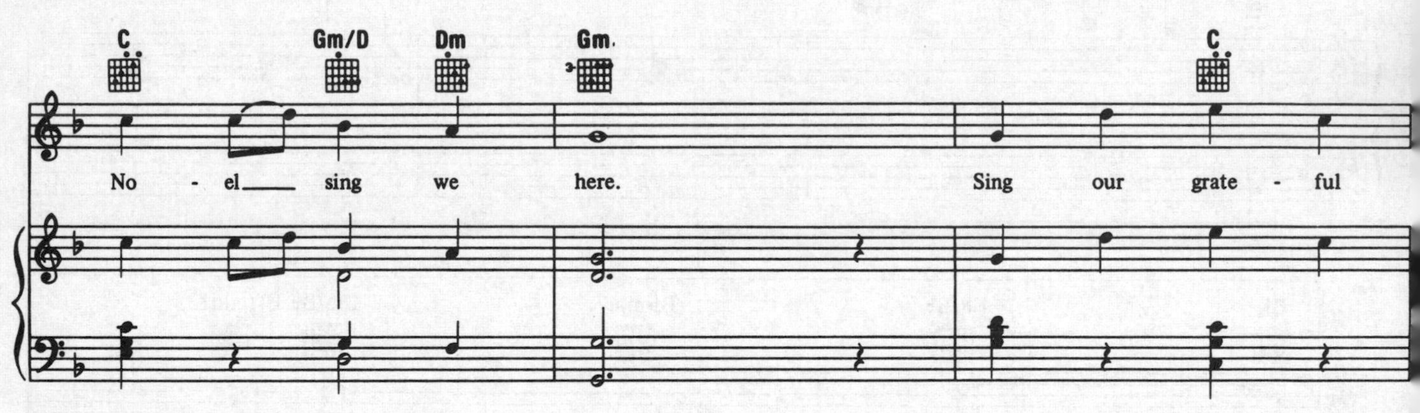
C
Gm/D
Dm
Gm
C
No - el sing we here. Sing our grate - ful

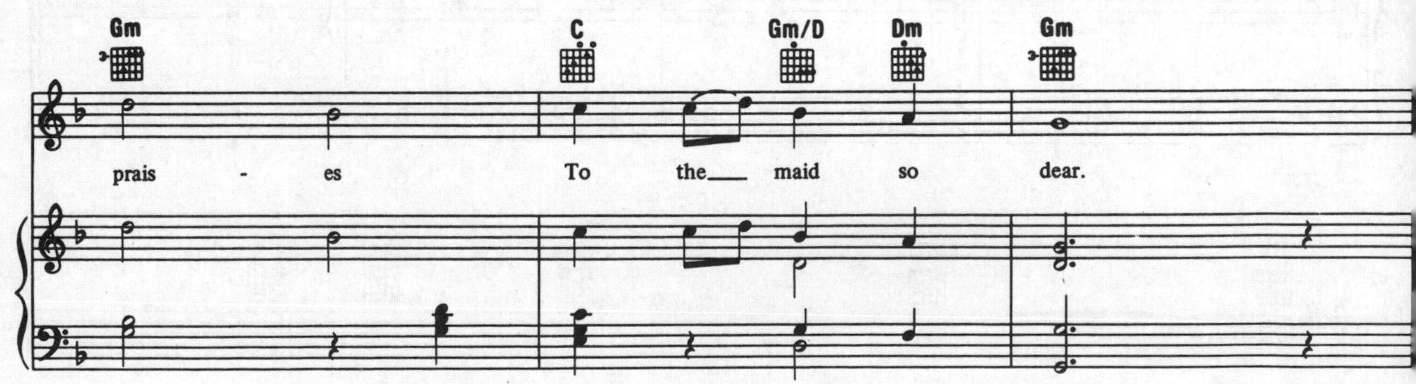
Gm
C
Gm/D
Dm
Gm
prais - es To the maid so dear.

Dm
Gm
Sing we No - el! The King is born. No -
Dm
Gm
C
Gm
el! Sing We Now Of Christ - mas,
C
Gm/D
Dm
Gm
C
Gm
C
Sing we here No - el. Sing We Now Of
Gm
C
Gm/D
Dm
Gm
C
Christ - mas, No - el sing we here.

Gm C Gm C Gm/D Dm
Sing our grate - ful prais - es To the maid so
Gm Dm
dear. Sing we No - el! The
Gm Dm Gm C
King is born. No - el! Sing We Now Of
Gm C Gm/D Dm Gm
Christ - mas, Sing we here No - el.

SOME CHILDREN SEE HIM

Lyric by WIHLA HUTSON
Music by ALFRED BURT

Slowly
F Bb F Dm Am Bb Am
Some Chil-dren See Him lil - y_ white, The Ba - by Je - sus_ born this night. Some
Some Chil-dren See Him al - mond_eyed, This Sav-iour whom we_ kneel be - side, Some
The Chil-dren in each dif - f'rent_place Will see the Ba - by_ Je - sus' face Like
Bb Am Gm F Gm Dm
Chil - dren See Him lil - y_ white, With tress - es soft and_ fair. Some
Chil - dren See Him al - mond_eyed, With skin of yel - low_ hue. Some
theirs, but bright with heav'n - ly_ grace, And filled with ho - ly_ light. O
C Dm7 Am Bb Gm Fm Gm7 C11
Chil - dren See Him_ bronzed and brown, The Lord of heav'n to_ earth come down; Some
Chil - dren See Him_ dark as they, Sweet Mar - y's Son to_ whom we pray; Some
lay a - side each_ earth - ly thing, And with thy heart as_ of - fer - ing, Come
F Bbm Bb Am7 Gm7 F
Chil - dren See Him bronzed and_ brown, With dark and heav - y_ hair.
Chil - dren See Him dark as_ they, And ah! they love him_ too!
wor - ship now the In - fant_ King, 'Tis love that's born to - night!

THE STAR CAROL

Lyric by WIHLA HUTSON
Music by ALFRED BURT

Tenderly with much expression

Eb Bb Eb Ab F7 Bb Bdim

Long years a - go on a deep__ win - ter night,
Je - sus, the Lord was that Ba - by so small,
Dear Ba - by Je - sus, how ti - ny Thou art,

mp

Cm G7 Cm Fm Dm7-5 G

High in the heav'ns a ___ star ___ shone bright,
Laid down to sleep in a hum - ble stall;
I'll make a place for ___ Thee __ in my heart,

Fm7 Gm Fm7 Gm Fm Gm Ebmaj7 Ab Gm7

While in a man - ger a wee in - fant lay,
Then came the star and it stood o - ver head,
And when the stars in the heav - ens I see,

Abmaj7 Ab Gm Fm7 Eb Ab6 Eb

Sweet - ly a - sleep on a bed of hay.
Shed - ding its light 'round His lit - tle bed.
Ev - er and al - ways I think of Thee.

WHAT CHILD IS THIS?

Words by WILLIAM C. DIX
16th Century English Melody

Moderately slow
Em
Am
F#m
Bm
F#7
B7
mp
What Child is this, who, laid to rest, on Ma - ry's lap is sleep -
lies He in such mean es - tate, where ox and ass are feed -
bring Him in - cense, gold, and myrrh, come, peas - ant, king to own

Em
Am
Em
ing? Whom an - gels greet with
ing? Good Chris - tian, fear; for
Him. The King of kings sal -
F#m
Bm
C
Bm
Am
an - thems sweet while shep - herds
sin - ners here the si - lent
va - tion brings, let bow - ing
B7
E
A
E
G
watch are keep - ing?
Word is plead - ing.
hearts en - throne Him.
This,
F#m
Bm
Em
this is Christ the King, whom shep - herds

F♯7
B
B7
guard and an - gels sing:
G
F♯m
Haste, haste to bring him
Bm
C
B7
laud, the babe, the son of
1,2
Am
Em
3
E
Ma - ry.
Why
So
Ma - ry.

STILL, STILL, STILL

Salzburg Melody, c.1819
Traditional Austrian Text

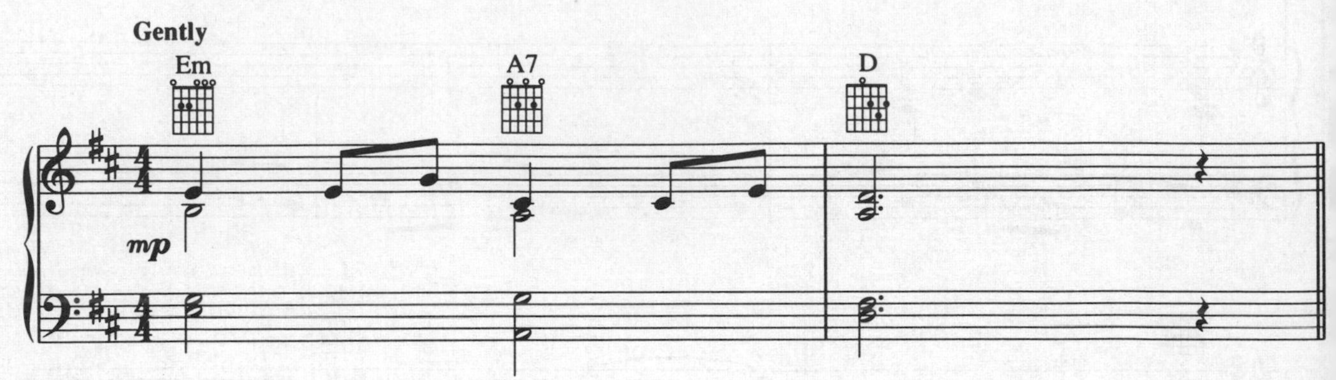
Gently
Em
A7
D
mp

Bm
Em
A7
Still, Still, still, To sleep is now His
Sleep, sleep, sleep, while we Thy vi - gil

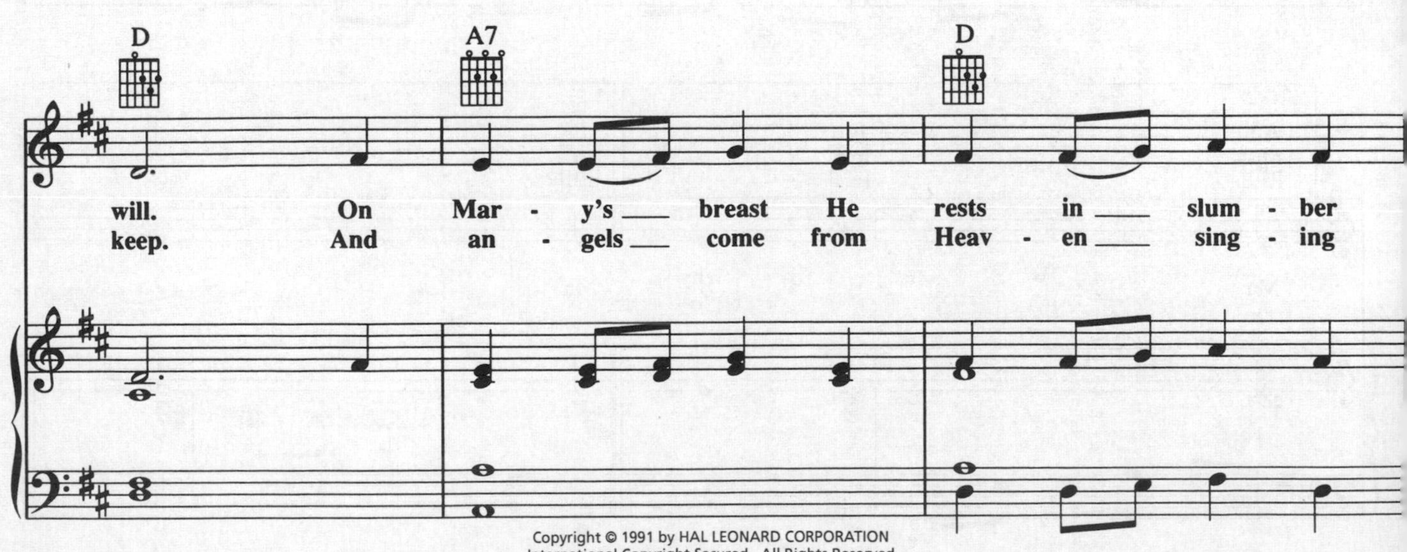
D
A7
D
will. On Mar - y's breast He rests in slum - ber
keep. And an - gels come from Heav - en sing - ing

A7
D
D/C#
while we pray in end - less num - ber. Still, still,
songs of ju - bi - la - tion bring - ing sleep, sleep,
Bm
Bm/A
Em/G
A7
1
D
still. To sleep is now His will.
sleep, while we Thy vi - gil
2
D
D/C#
Bm
Bm/A
keep. Sleep, sleep, sleep, while
Em/G
A7
D
we Thy vi - gil keep.
rall.

THERE'S A SONG IN THE AIR

Words and Music by JOSIAH G. HOLLAND
and KARL P. HARRINGTON

Flowing
C6
Cm/E♭
G/D
D7
G
mf
1. There's a
2. There's a
song in the air! There's a star in the
tu - mult of joy O'er the won - der - ful
D7/A
G/B
D7
G/B
Gm6/B♭
D/A
sky! There's a moth - er's deep prayer And a
birth, For the vir - gin's sweet boy Is the

A7
D
G
D7/A
G/B
ba - by's low cry!
Lord of the earth.
And the star rains its
Am/C
G/B
C
D7
D7/C
D7/A
D7
G9
fire while the beau - ti - ful sing,
For the man - ger of
C6
Cm6/E♭
G/D
A7
D7
G
Beth - le - hem cra - dles a King!

3. In the light of that star
Lie the ages impearled,
And that song from afar
Has swept over the world.
Ev'ry hearth is aflame, and the angels sing,
In the homes of the nations that Jesus is King!

4. We rejoice in the light,
And we echo the song
That comes down thro' the night
From the heavenly throng.
Ay! we shout to the lovely evangel they bring
And we greet in His cradle our Savior and King!

UP ON THE HOUSETOP

Words and Music by
B.R. HANDY

Brightly
E♭
Edim
Fm7
B♭7
E♭
Edim
mf
Fm7
B♭7
E♭
Up on the house - top rein - deer pause,
First comes the stock - ing of lit - tle Nell;
A♭
E♭/G
B♭7
Out jumps good old San - ta Claus;
Oh, dear San - ta, fill it well;
E♭
Down thru the chim - ney with lots of toys,
Give her a dol - lie that laughs and cries,

A♭
E♭/G
B♭7
E♭
All for the lit - tle ones, Christ - mas joys.
One that will o - pen and shut her eyes.
3
A♭
E♭
B♭7
Ho, ho, ho! Who would - n't go! Ho, ho, ho!
E♭
E♭/D♭
A♭/C
E♭/B♭
A♭
Who would - n't go!
Up on the house - top, click, click, click,
E♭
E♭/G
B♭7
E♭
Down thru the chim - ney with good Saint Nick.

WE NEED A LITTLE CHRISTMAS

from MAME

Music and Lyric by
JERRY HERMAN

Brightly (as a polka)
mf
Chorus
G
G6
Gmaj7
G6
1. Haul out the hol - ly, Put up the
climb down the chim - ney, Turn on the
mp-mf
G
G6
Gmaj7
G6
Dm6
E7
E7-9
Am7
tree be - fore my spir - it falls a - gain; Fill
bright - est string of lights I've ev - er seen; Slice
D7
Am
Am7
D7
Am7
Am7-5
up the stock - ing, I may be rush - ing things, but
up the fruit - cake, It's time we hung some tin - sel

D7 Dm6 E7
deck the halls a - gain now.
on that ev - er - green bough.
Am6 E7 Am D7 G Gmaj7 G6 G+ G
For We Need A Lit - tle Christ - mas, Right this ver - y min - ute,
For I've grown a lit - tle lean - er, Grown a lit - tle cold - er,
3. For we need a lit - tle mu - sic, Need a lit - tle laugh - ter,
Am D7 G Gmaj7 G6 G7 C
Can - dles in the win - dow, Car - ols at the spin - et. Yes, We Need A Lit - tle
Grown a lit - tle sad - der, Grown a lit - tle old - er. And I need a lit - tle
Need a lit - tle sing - ing Ring - ing through the raft - er. And we need a lit - tle
D7 G Gmaj7 G6 A7
Christ - mas, Right this ver - y min - ute, It has - n't snowed a sin - gle flur - ry, But
an - gel, Sit - ting on my shoul - der, I
snap - py "hap - py ev - er af - ter," We
D7 Am D9 D7 G
D.S. to 3rd Lyric
San - ta, dear, we're in a hur - ry. 2. So Need A Lit - tle Christ - mas now!
sf

WE THREE KINGS OF ORIENT ARE

Words and Music by
JOHN H. HOPKINS, JR.

Moderately
mp
Em
B7
Em
We Three Kings of O - ri - ent are;
B7
Em
Bear - ing gifts we tra - verse a - far,
D
G
Field and foun - tain, moor and moun - tain,

Am
Em/B
B7
Em
D7
Fol - low - ing yon - der star. O
G
C
G
star of won - der, star of night,
C
G
Star with roy - al beau - ty bright,
Em
D
G
C
G
D
G
West - ward lead - ing, still pro - ceed - ing,
C
G
Guide us to thy per - fect light.

WHAT CHRISTMAS MEANS TO ME

Words and Music by GEORGE GORDY,
ALLEN STORY and ANNA GORDY GAYE

Brightly
N.C.
mf
C
F
Can - dles burn - in' low,
C
F
C
lots of mis - tle - toe,
lots of snow — and ice,

F
C
F
ev - 'ry - where we go.
C
F
C
Choirs sing - in' car - ols right out - side my
F
Dm7
door. All these things and more,
F/G
that's what Christ - mas means to me,
(All these things and more, ba - by.)

my love. (That's what Christ - mas means to me, my love.)
N.C.
C
F
I see your smil - ing face like I
C
F
C
nev - er seen be - fore. E - ven though I love

F
C
F
you mad - ly, it seems I love you more.
The lit -
C
F
tle cards you'll give me will touch
C
F
Dm7
my heart for sure.
All these things and more,
dar - lin',
that's what Christ -
(All these things and more, dar - lin'.)

F/G
- mas means to me my love. (That's what
Christ - mas means to me, my love.)
F
I feel like run -
- nin' wild,
as anx - ious as a lit - tle child to greet
C
you 'neath the mis - tle - toe,
kiss you once and then

F
Dm
some more. And wish you a mer - ry Christ - mas, ba - by,
F/G
and such hap - pi - ness in the com -
(Wish you a mer - ry Christ - mas ba - by.)
G♭/A♭
- ing year. Whoa, ba -
D♭
- by. Let's deck the halls with hol -

Gb
Db
Gb
- ly,
sing sweet "Si - lent Night."
Db
Gb
Db
Fill a tree with an - gel hair and pret - ty, pret - ty lights.
Gb
Db
Gb
Go to sleep and wake up
Db
Gb
Ebm7
just be - fore day - light.
And all these things and more,

baby,
(All these things and more, baby.)
that's what Christ-mas means to me, my love. (That's what
Christ-mas means to me, my love.)
G♭/A♭
D♭
G♭
D♭
G♭
Repeat ad lib. and Fade
Optional Ending
D♭

WHILE SHEPHERDS WATCHED THEIR FLOCKS

Words by NAHUM TATE
Music by GEORGE FRIDERIC HANDEL
Moderately
mf
C F C
While_ shep - herds watched their flocks by _ night, All _ seat - ed on the _
C/G G G7 C
ground, _ The _ an - gel of the Lord came_ down, and
F C/E G7/D C F/C C F C/G C/G C
glo - ry shone a - round, _ And glo - ry shone a - round.

WHO WOULD IMAGINE A KING

from the Touchstone Motion Picture THE PREACHER'S WIFE

Words and Music by MERVYN WARREN
and HALLERIN HILTON HILL

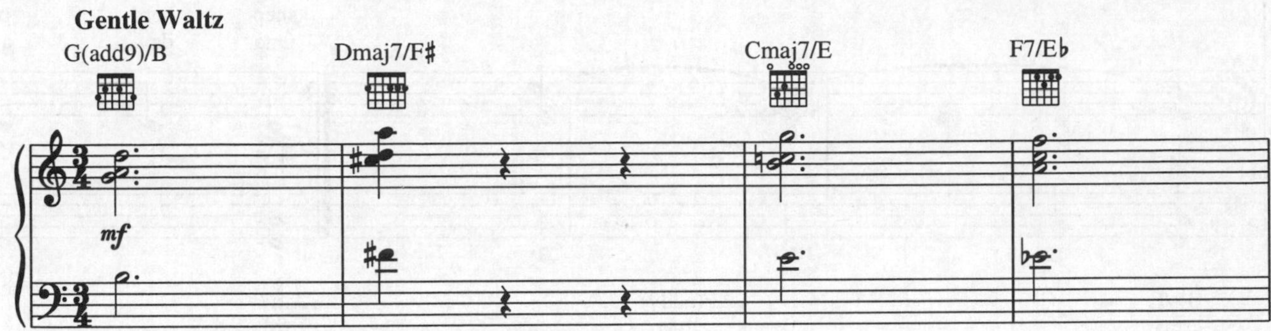
Gentle Waltz
G(add9)/B
Dmaj7/F#
Cmaj7/E
F7/Eb
mf

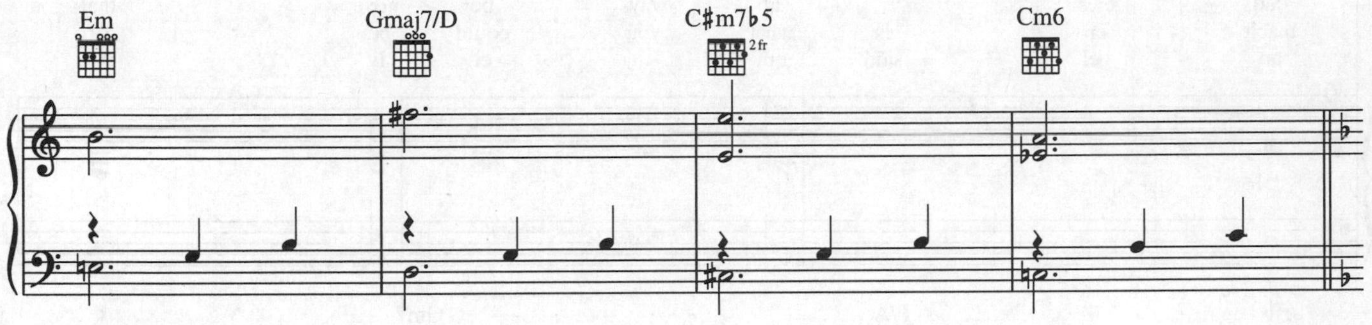
Em
Gmaj7/D
C#m7b5
2fr
Cm6

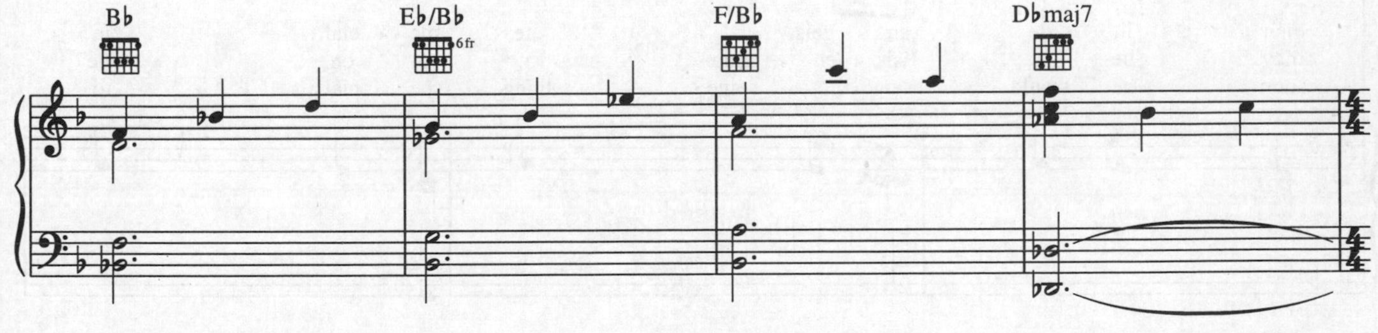
Bb
Eb/Bb
6fr
F/Bb
Dbmaj7

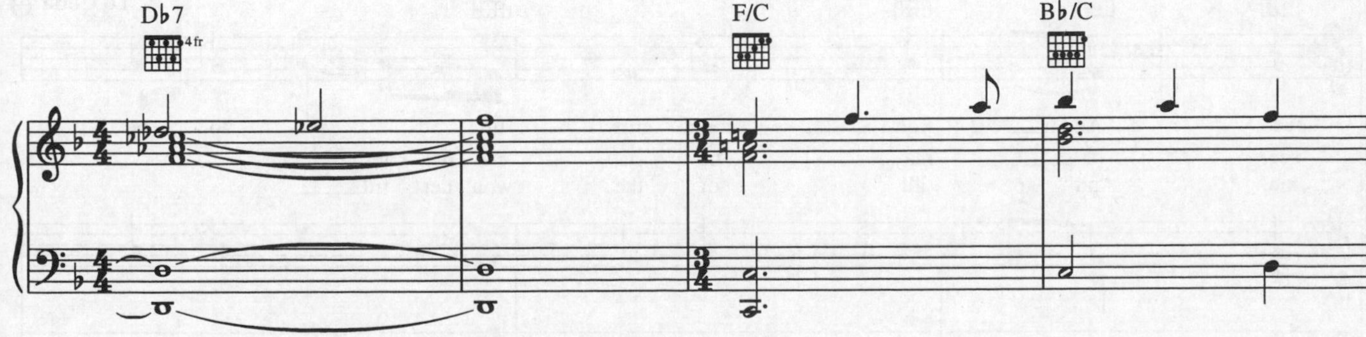
Db7
4fr
F/C
Bb/C

C6
B♭6/9
Gm7
D♭maj9
B♭/C
F(add9)
Mom - mies and
shep - herd or
One day, an
B♭/F
F(add9)
Am7
dad - dies al - ways be - lieve that
teach - er is what you could be, or
an - gel said qui - et - ly that
B♭
F/A
Gm7
their lit - tle an - gels are spe - cial in -
may - be a fish - er - man out on the
soon he would bring some - thing spe - cial to
B♭/C
C♯dim7
Dm7
Dm7/C
To Coda
deed. And you could grow up to be
sea, or may - be a car - pen - ter
me. And of all of the won - der - ful

B♭maj7
Gm7♭5
5fr
F/C
B♭/C
an - y - thing.
build - ing things.
But who would i - mag - ine a
1
F(add9)
B♭(add9)
6fr
C/F
2
F
King?
A
King?
Fmaj7/G
G7
B♭/C
C7
It was so clear when the
F/C
A♭dim7/C
B♭/C
C7
wise men ar - rived and the an - gels were sing - ing your

Fmaj7
Fmaj7/G
G7
B♭/C
name
that the world would be
C♯dim7
Dm7
Dm7/C
dif - f'rent 'cause you were a - live. That's why
D♭
B♭m7
B♭/C
heav - en stood still to pro - claim.
D.S. al Coda
CODA
Bm7♭5
B♭m6
6fr
gifts he could bring,
rit.

F/C
A7♯5
Dm7
who would i - mag - ine, who could i - mag -
E♭9
F/C
B♭/C
- ine, who would i - mag - ine a
F
E♭/F
B♭(add2)/F
King?
B♭m6
6fr
F(add9)
6
Mm.
6

WONDERFUL CHRISTMASTIME

Words and Music by
McCARTNEY

Brightly
Cm7
Dm
E♭
A♭9
B♭
mf
B♭
B♭maj7
B♭
Gm/B♭
The mood is right, the spir-it's up,
The par-ty's on the feel-ing's here
The word is out a-bout the town,
B♭
F/B♭
B♭
we're here to-night and that's e-nough.
that on-ly comes this time of year.
to lift a glass, oh don't look down.
Cm7
Cm7/F
F7/D
Gm9
E♭
A♭9
B♭
Sim-ply hav-ing a won-der-ful Christ-mas-time.

Cm7
Cm7/F
F7/D
Gm9
E♭
A♭9
1
B♭
Sim - ply hav - ing a won - der - ful Christ - mas - time.
2,3
B♭
Gm
Cm7
time.
The choir of chil - dren
The choir of chil - dren
F7
B♭
Gm
Cm7
sing their song.
sing their song. (They prac - tised all year
F7
To Coda
B♭
Ding dong, ding dong. Ding
long.)

E♭
Cm7
dong, ding.
Ooh
Ooh.
E♭/B♭
E♭
B♭/D
Do do do
B♭
B♭maj7
B♭
Gm/B♭
do do do do.
B♭
F/B♭
B♭

Cm7
Cm7/F
F7/D
Gm9
E♭
A♭9
We're sim - ply hav - ing a won - der - ful Christ - mas -
B♭
time. Sim - ply hav - ing a won - der - ful Christ - mas -
D.S. al Coda
time.
CODA
E♭/B♭
Ding dong, ding dong, ding
dong, ding dong, ding dong, ding dong, dong
F7

B♭
B♭maj7
B♭
Gm/B♭
dong, dong, dong. The par - ty's on, the spir-it's up,
B♭
B♭maj9
we're here to-night
B♭
Cm7
Cm7/F
and that's e-nough.
Sim - ply
sim - ply
F7/D
Gm9
E♭
A♭9
B♭
Repeat and Fade
hav - ing a won - der - ful Christ - mas - time. We're
hav - ing a won - der - ful Christ - mas - time.